The Prophet In The Wilderness

Ken Cox

REJOICE
Essential Publishing

Much love to you! Mary, God has a work for you to do

KC

All rights reserved
Rejoice Essential Publishing
P.O. BOX 85
Bennettsville, SC 29512
www.republishing.org

Visit the author's website at www.whereeaglesfly.us

The Prophet In The Wilderness/ Ken Cox

ISBN-10: 1-946756-10-5
ISBN-13: 978-1-946756-10-7

Library of Congress Control Number: 2017947597

Dedication

My very special thanks to my wife, Prophetess Sabina Cox, who has stuck with me through thick and thin and showed me love, understanding, and most of all a necessary prophetic trait called patience. She is the reason I'm where I am today as she constantly educated and worked with me on acceptable standards of myself and those to whom God assigned to Where Eagles Fly Fellowship and Ministries, Inc. She has been and is my non-public prophetic voice and seer. To our Children, CJ, Arlina, and Kenneth Cox Jr. (AKA The Nature Boy) to their spouses and our Grandchildren, I say a heartfelt I love and thank you. I have been gone, and away at times on the battlefield for God and missed key events in your lives and I must say each one of you have been in my thoughts and prayers and I'm forever grateful to each of you for that, I humbly say thank you so much.

I also want to thank every leader who has input into my life and those who continue to do so, they are simply too numerous to mention but they know who they are. On a personal note, my parents, The late Dr. Rev. Tommy Eugene Cox and my mom, The Late Arvella Brunson and My stepdad, The Late Freddie Brunson, all played a significant role in my life and each one of them has given me something that I will forever be indebted to them and thank God for their work in my life. My Grandmother, the late Golena Everette, who religiously took me and my brothers to church across the street from my mother's house and taught us constantly about simply knowing God. I don't have the words to adequately express my thoughts.

While they are gone, I'm still blessed to have my God mother, "Cousin" Grace Malloy to talk with and counsel with as well as My Apostolic Father, Apostle Centry Prince and Apostolic mother, Apostle Willie Rhaines. These 3 people have played a major role in my life. To those who know me on a personal level and have spent time with me imparting the kingdom into my life, I offer my most humble thank you.

Each prophet of God goes through a journey, no two are the same, as we are all different people, but yet there is a high calling that alerts our inner man and sets us apart for the work of God as his Spiritual specialists. We are his chosen servants, the Prophets.

Contents

CHAPTER ONE

Introduction

In every life we struggle and wonder who we are, and then comes the moment we realize something about ourselves, our life, our surroundings and most of all our purpose. We come to understand what we can live with, who we are, and what we are willing to defend until the very end of our life. My moment came right before I met Prophetess Cox, as I was struggling to start over again from what appeared to be another failed relationship. What I did not know was that I was being placed and positioned for greatness. I will make no excuses to you, I have lived life much as many of you, with a bevy of failures and seemly a dysfunctional burden. I often wondered how God would use me in a mess of crap that appeared as my life. My process was coming full circle just like yours.

I found out that my processing was beginning and what was and took the appearance of drama, and seemingly bad luck, was my preparation for the prophetic ministry. I value the time of my initial processing, and hopefully by the end of this book, you will value yours. I have been led to share with you much of the information I have experienced and learned, as I continue to evolve as a prophet sent to the nations. I can't help but still be amazed at the plan of God in my life. I take a great honor to welcome you to The Prophet in the Wilderness.

This will be our unique opportunity to explore our life and learn from God's greatest prophets who will take us through our personal processing and allow us to see that we all are still works in progress. We know that this is a constant and ongoing process and as we process from the wilderness to the front lines for God, we learn that the struggle is not just on us or even about us. The struggle is about you and I being prepared as a soldier prepares for battle. The struggle, as you will see, is our process. One thing I must warn you about as you read this book, you are still processing; you are still being developed for even greater works.

My aim is to sharpen your prophetic mentality. There clearly is a lack of adequate mentality for continual sustained success in the prophetic. We see people come and go, on fire for God on Monday and totally lost by Wednesday at lunchtime. Why? That's a fair and a good question to ask. In Genesis 37 we see the start of the life of Joseph, who was to become a prophetic standard for prophetic mentality. Joseph shows us there is a purpose for our problems, our ups as downs, as we move into the sea of life. Joseph finally came out of his wilderness; what about us?

The wilderness can simply be defined as issues in your life that are a product of economic, social and spiritual factors in your life. The prophet on the west coast has a different reality from the prophet on the east coast and vice versa. There seems to be no clear cut standards in the prophetic ministry as we see in other five-fold offices such as pastor and evangelist or even the teacher. Yes, we are putting more attention and work into developing the gifts, but the disconnect between prophetic teachers and prophets of different lineages is frightening and dysfunctional. As prophets these are some things we don't admit openly. We know we have a lack of functionally within our prophetic relationships, but I thank God for all the senior prophets who are working daily to alleviate these issues and allow all who want to grow to do just that - grow!

There may always be that group or contingent who looks at us and say that the prophet is dead, and the Apostle too. They may continue to feel this way, even if they see signs and wonders from the work of God. They must realize we are not chosen to be man's prophets, but God's Servants - his prophets. I'm not even surprised to know some will, and still secretly of course, consult a psychic, but openly say the prophets are dead.

My challenge extends to you as you read this and become effective in your calling for God. This work is dedicated to you and the question of what's next? You're a prophet in the wilderness. Let's see how to answer the question for your life.

CHAPTER TWO

What Is The Prophetic Ministry?

"Communicating The Will And Mind Of God."

One of the most critical things the prophet in the wilderness must understand is why they exist. There will be times we will find ourselves going through a wilderness experience. The wilderness is where most prophets discover their gift. Our prophetic gift is from God and its purpose is to provide a way for man to speak forth the mind and counsel of God for repentance to be taught and righteousness to preached in order to bring restoration, to heal (Matthew 4:34; 9:35), "for the testimony of Jesus is the spirit of prophecy." "... for the substance (essence) of the truth revealed by Jesus is the spirit of all prophecy" (Revelation 19:10).

Prophetic ministry also provides a way for the priorities, the present-day utility of God's power, and contemporary purposes to be communicated to man as history progresses.

Amos 3:7 "Surely the Lord God will do nothing, but he revealeth his secret unto his servants the prophets."

Hebrews 1:1,2 "God, who at sundry times and in divers manners spake in time past unto the fathers by the prophets, Hath in these last days spoken unto us by his Son, whom he hath appointed heir of all things, by whom also he made the worlds"

Revelation 10:7 "But in the days of the voice of the seventh angel, when he shall begin to sound, the mystery of God should be finished, as he hath declared to his servants the prophets."

There has never been a situation in this world that a prophet somewhere did not know or was aware of. Imagine how many prophets knew of 9/11 and yet were ignored. This is the substance that frustrates today's prophets as they look for their best efforts to yield fruit and yet they seem to get ignored, often constantly.

God is restoring the prophetic ministry to the church as never seen before. Prophets are springing up from everywhere and people are more than ever aware of the prophetic ministry as never before. Understand that today you are part of a remnant of prophets that God is raising up right before our eyes.

This situation, which is quite new to the church in these days and times, leads to many questions. While the prophetic anointing also gives men the ability to speak unto other men a word of exhortation, comfort and revelation (1 Corinthians 14:3;30), we need to understand the church of today is still not totally sold on us, nor are we totally sold on them. Thank God for his divine connections, divine assignments, and special anointed prophets who he uses to bridge this gap between prophets and the church.

Questions about prophets still abound. Church member as well as those called to the prophetic ministry have questions. Some of the daily questions are:

What is the prophetic ministry? What is the purpose and function of the prophetic ministry in the church today? What is a prophet? What does the word prophetic actually means? What about someone who prophesies every Sunday in church, is he or she a prophet? How do I know that I am really called to the prophetic ministry? What are the signs that I should look for? If I am called to the prophetic ministry how will it be manifested in me? How will God train me? What sort of preparation will I have to go through? How long does it take to be trained as a prophet?

Prophets and all perspective prophetic people, if the Lord has called you and you would like to be trained, then apply to be a student and you will have the answers to all these questions during your training. Prophets are God's spiritual specialists.

The amazing thing is that many want to treat being a prophet like a 9-5 job in which the perspective prophet wants all information upfront. This is not a job, this is a lifestyle, with a call unto your death.

When we look at the word "prophetic" we learn that it is an adjective related to two words prophecy and prophet.[1] Prophecy[2]: is defined as a discourse or speech, emanating from divine inspiration and declaring the purposes of God, whether by reproving and admonishing the wicked, or comforting the afflicted, or revealing things hidden; esp. by foretelling future events. This is what we do as prophets. This is our work and whatever else God says. The term prophet is one who, moved by the Spirit of God and is hence his spokesman or spokeswoman[3], solemnly declares to men what he has received by inspiration, especially concerning future events. In particular they declare things as they relate to the cause and kingdom of God.

We need to remember here that prophecy involves an utterance or communication through words or actions. The prophetic ministry involves speaking ahead of what God is planning to do. It can also involve preparing the ground for what God is planning to do. I'm telling you this because in the wilderness, we are processed to become prophets of God. Our utterance actually covers a lot of what goes as normal preaching. We are prophets with an uncommon utterance under the inspiration of God. We are exercising the prophetic ministry when we utter what God is saying to others under inspiration of God.

Please understand that the prophetic can also fall under inspired preaching, but it is of course a lot more than that. People may be tempted to believe that a prophet is someone who just has a gift of prophecy or who prophesies. But the prophetic ministry is actually more. A prophet has a mandate from God to equip the saints to do the work of the Lord. This is why we must train; we must work together and learn more about our gifts.

Today we have prophets and lay people who get confused. The confusion comes from the failure to distinguish between three biblical concepts: gifts of the spirit, body of Christ ministries, and leadership ministries referred to as the fivefold ministry.

The body of Christ ministries are found in Roman 12:4-8 and include: prophecy, servanthood, teaching, exhortation and encouragement, giving to others and meeting their needs, taking charge or leading others, compassion and mercy, and taking care of people. These are ministries that every single member of the body of Christ is called to function and operate in. Every believer has got a ministry because the word ministry simply means service, so to minister means to serve. There is no special training needed. Believers receive from the Lord and function naturally.

The five-fold leadership ministries are found in Ephesians 4:11 and are: apostles, prophets, teachers, evangelists, and pastors. These are the governing body of the church. The ministry of the prophet is found here.

The gifts of the spirit (Romans 12:6–8, 1 Corinthians 12:8–10, 1 Peter 4:11) are tools and abilities that the Lord has given his servants to carry out successfully their functions in the church. Since we have both body of Christ ministries and five-fold ministries, the spiritual gifts are available to ministries to carry out their functions and serve the Lord efficiently.

Understand that a person in the body of Christ may have the 'body of Christ ministry of prophecy' and will need the need the gift of prophecy to carry out that ministry; likewise the prophet will need the same gift of prophecy. They relate to the prophetic. The latter involves more than just prophesying. This means that a person with the body of Christ ministry of prophecy, or the gift of prophecy, may carry out a prophetic ministry but they are not a prophet. Prophets on the other hand can not only prophesy but also carry out many other functions. We need to learn this. For example, the ministry of exhortation is also a prophetic function. Although it is not prophetic in itself, the prophetic ministry is usually designed to motivate and encourage believers to go on with God and to find their place in the body.

There are some functions that set prophets apart such as having two or more of the revelatory gifts listed in 1 Corinthians 12. These gifts will be discussed in more detail below. The prophetic ministry is to bring the body of Christ to place of maturity. The only way to know that the body of Christ is at a place of maturity is when believers are walking in faith, love and hope. There is no substitute for this. The prophet is to bring believers to a full knowledge of the Lord and help prepare believers for the ministry God has called them to do.

Prophets in the fulfillment of the prophetic ministry, will need some specific spiritual gifts called "prophetic gifts". They are the vocal, revelation and power gifts. There are three groups of spiritual gifts mentioned in 1 Corinthians 12: the vocal gifts (prophecy, diverse tongues, interpretation of tongues), the revelation gifts (word of knowledge, word of wisdom, discerning of spirits) and the power gifts (faith, miracles, healings). The vocal gift of prophecy, is the most obvious one since most people believe that all a prophet does is prophesy. So the prophetic gifts are given to the prophet in order to fulfill a specific goal or their God ordained assignment.

The main power gift of the prophetic ministry is the gift of faith. Without this gift the prophet cannot function properly. We just don't predict, we are part of the solution to whatever problem God reveals through them. This is why the prophetic decrees are important. Today's prophets must understand that when we seem to have a problem, the decree is not enough. Faith makes it effective. Over and over again, we see the prophets of God making decrees covered by faith. This is relationship of faith and the prophetic to its fullest. God can use prophets in the other power gifts which is gift of healings and gift of working of miracles.

A prophet needs to do more than prophesying. We need to send forth prophetic decrees so that whatever the Lord is planning for the individual or the body of Christ to come to pass will be known. Prophets, while ministering directly to a person or in prayer, can send forth a prophetic decree and become part of the solution of whatever the person is expecting. Faith is the supernatural force which, when released into the earth, accomplishes the will of and purposes of God. So as the prophet decrees, the gift of faith is released to accomplish the will of God. The prophet fulfills this function mainly through intercession. This is how God uses us.

What about the gifts of wisdom and the prophet? We are tasked to equip the saints for the work of ministry. We do this as we help them to identify their gifts and ministries, and the main tool is the gift of the word of wisdom. Wisdom will allow us as prophets to reveal what ministry they are called to and point them in the direction to go further by giving them encouragement and direction on how to grow in that ministry. Believers will have revelations or some impressions regarding their calling that they don't understand. The prophet can use the word of wisdom to bring confirmation. When the prophet does this, they really build hope in the lives of believers; they give them something to hang onto and something to live for. That's part of our job as prophets of God. Here again, we need to be processed ourselves in order to be effective.

The prophetic ministry, when employed, will speak words of exhortation, comfort and revelation. Encouragement and edification are birthed through a prophetic word. A word that tell believers how much God loves them and how valuable they are to Him will certainly bring them closer to the Lord. There is individual and corporate edification, learning and comfort. This is what the public usage exercise of the prophetic gift must do and that is to be a sign and direction for believers. As prophets we use prophecy to encourage and edify the body of Christ.

A seasoned and mature prophetic ministry should always seek to mature the saints by preparing them for the works of God's assignments and teaching them how to build up the body of Christ. Its purpose is to bring about unity of the faith that comes with the knowledge of the Son of God so that the body of Christ will mature into the full measure of Christ Himself.

A prophetic ministry will continue to help the body of Christ grow in understanding and knowledge of that which has already been written for us in the Bible, the word of God. True prophetic ministry will always point to the true unity of the faith to the Glory of God, based upon the knowledge of the Son of God, which comes from the truth of the word of God which teaches us of Christ. It will emphasize that unity in the body of Christ must be based upon the truth of scripture.

The true prophet of God understands that their influence over others only comes when and if they voluntarily and willingly follow their example of personal holiness and servanthood to others by their service to God.

How do we identify authentic prophetic ministry? This answer will vary but let's tackle this and look at the biblical options, as we can't go wrong. There is a call to repentance. Prophetic ministry will address sin. Let's look at Haggai 1:2-9 and Zechariah 1:3-4. The prophet Haggai challenged Israel to consider their ways, specifically their complacency regarding the Lord's house and their zeal regarding their own houses and possessions.

The Prophet Zechariah confronted their apostasy, encouraging them to repent and return to the Lord. Without a doubt, this type of bold confrontation of sin must be the norm before we will ever witness the depth of profound repentance necessary to turn the church around and the world upside down. As prophets, we are able to communicate that the voice of the Lord is different from man's voice. The Prophet Haggai made a distinction between the Lord's words and his own words. Today it is easy to see that not all who say "Thus saith the Lord" speak for God. It is no secret that some prophesy as a means to gain popularity and prosperity or to promote their doctrine.

True prophetic ministry will yield this kind of fruit; prophets who delight themselves in the fear of the Lord partake of that same spirit by dwelling in the secret place of the Most High. Without the spirit of the fear of the Lord, repentance has about the same effect as brow beating.

One major problem many of us have is that we automatically turn a deaf ear to the Lord's command of 2 Chronicles. 7:14. We, especially prophets, must humble ourselves, pray, seek His face and turn from our wicked ways. we have found ourselves in a spiritual wilderness and our land is in need of much healing. How are we going help anyone if we are still in the wilderness?

When we come out of the wilderness, we can speak boldly break out of the bondage and eliminate the excuses that keep us from pushing forward toward the mark for the prize of the high calling of God in Christ Jesus as we see in Ezra 6:14.

Haggai prophesied that the glory of the latter temple would be greater than the former. Your prophetic ministry should point me towards God always. We see much of prophetic ministry today is associated with private agenda instead of God's purposes.

We have sold out to the heart of man rather than what is on God's heart. Prophetic ministry must begin with a burden from the Lord that finds expression through soul travel and a burning word from heaven that cannot be contained. All prophets must learn this in the wilderness as we dwell in the secret place with the Most High (Jeremiah. 20:9).

CHAPTER THREE

Jumping Into Your Prophetic Process

"What Is It You Must Do?"

Every prophet is endowed with some special skill when born. If you want to be successful, you need to find your gift and embrace it and jump into the process of your prophetic development.

When we see prophets and people in life as they stand on the cliff of life not being productive, we also see people soaring by who are. Funny how we see God using prophets. You see them traveling and continually doing the work of God, or maybe you look up and see the mega prosperity in a certain area of ministry or on a prophets life and you ask a question "How are they doing that?"

Have you ever wondered, 'Maybe this prophet has identified their gift and is living in their gifting assignment?' Believe it or not, every successful prophet in the body of Christ has been through God's initial special processing for their unique gift. Prophet, you cannot just exist in this life. You have got to learn how to live. God has birthed you to live. If you're thinking there has got to be more in your life than there is, you're right. Prophets, to ascend to your next level, you're going to have to jump into the process.

Your secular education is only going to take you so far, but your gift is the only way you're going to soar as an eagle. Prophet, your gift is the foundation of your prophetic DNA. Your gifting demands will allow you to simply jump into the process if you're willing to trust God. Unless you jump into the process, your gift that is packed and not activated will never work orbe avail able to you because of your lack of confidence. You must jump into the process.

You were not just born to just survive; you were born to serve in a special capacity for God. Prophet, if not you're going to serve, it's simple: you'll be just existing. At some point and time before it's too late, the prayer is that you'll yearn and need to see and understand God's plan for you.

The biggest issue is how and what do I do and when do I do it? You need to know it will not be easy. Prophet as you pursue your development of your gift through God, understand that you're probably not going to succeed right away because you're being processed. It's going to take time, and you'll hit plenty of snags, but that doesn't mean you give up right away. You will come to understand that you are in a process that will challenge and change you.

When you first jump into the process, not much will function right in your life. You will be ridiculed and persecuted, you will suffer injury and you will hit rock bottom or your valley of 'dry bones'. Your soul will be wounded and you will suffer some physical scars but despite your injuries, eventually you will fall in Love with the process and you won't quit because you know that is not an option.

Prophet, if you ever want to get there, you're going to have to jump into the process. You can play it safe and deal without the cuts and the tears and you can stand on that cliff for life, forever safe, but if you don't jump into the process, you will never realize who or whose you are.

You have a gift, don't waste it. Your prophetic gift is a supernatural ability given that needs to be discovered and developed. It is for the purpose of edifying the body of Christ.

The issue that most people in the prophetic have in dealing with the body of Christ is seen in this example. It's not a secret that a corporate church stands at the opposite end of the spectrum from a prophetic movement. Buildings, employees, assets, education, and retirement plans—all the things that can be threatened by instability. Some corporate churches view the prophetic as unstable. To have a prophet or prophets would be more of a problem than an asset. Trust that. So they see no point in God's activating the gift of prophecy among themselves. This is the unspoken doctrine of many traditional denominations today, especially concerning the prophets or apostles when their gifting is an issue.

To elevate this, anyone who has claimed to be a prophet would be met with skepticism by most. It's funny how people don't like the fact that prophets will likely tell you to do things differently than you have been. We as prophets have to be critical of church leaders. Imagine, who wants to receive us as a prophet who has or will identify our sins and shortcomings, as Bible prophets did? Sin will not be tolerated. Lay people wouldn't like it any better.

Even those of us who may agree with the prophet's message still and will wonder if change would be implemented if a prophet spoke it. Is the respect there and do you as a prophet believe that you are a true prophet? Or are we too sophisticated and too analytical in our thinking like most prophets? We don't develop simply because of the way we think. We like to look for holes in the prophet's message, not to mention the prophet's life.

Some church leaders will simply do their best to ignore a prophet. This is especially true if you are new. They do it as long as possible in the so-called truth of discerning your spirit.

We see a demonstration of attitude change when a seed is sown directly into some leaders in the pastor position. It is simply amazing how they label the prophet as money hungry, and a $50.00 or $100.00 bill in some leaders pockets will change a mindset about the prophet. This is simply a demonstration of the fickle nature of how some pastors and leaders see prophets. Thank God all are not like that, but what's a bigger disgrace is that some prophets have fallen for this trick.

So in our digression into the corporate type church of denominations, we see a church that is a self-protective church, a proud church, and, of course, the church that already has the whole truth. This is also a church with much to lose, and every one of them will tell you, not openly but selectivity, they can't host a prophet. God's prophets seemly are always in opposition to the organized church of their day; not much has changed as we look at where we are today with the diversity of leadership in today's churches.

True prophets will oppose things, and no one likes to be opposed. Jesus mentioned the persecution of the prophets several times (such as in Matthew 23:29–31), always with a finger pointing at the religious leaders. Have you ever noticed that many of today's leaders will stick with the dead prophets as they know people are more comfortable with them. No wonder they say we are dead! Let's not kid ourselves here, but it is what it is.

While we can look and see the theological reason for the diminishing state or the lack of the prophetic gift, in their opinion, it still remains an open question. It is so funny how many of the modern evangelicalism movements hold that the gift of prophecy has passed away completely, except when a resource is needed. They then remember we are prophets then. Some have chosen to modify our present-day prophetic movement with preaching or teaching. They identify us that way, but can't relate to our gifting. The good news is that God has anointed us to be part of the five-fold ministry for his purposes! Prophets, lets jump into our prophetic process and experience God in a whole new way.

CHAPTER FOUR

Why Prophets Run From Ministry to Ministry

"Moving From One Prophetic Ministry To Another"

Can you imagine Elijah who is exhilarated by his success on Mt. Carmel, and who also "outran Ahab to Jezreel (1 Kings 18:46)," a distance of about twenty-five miles. (Keep in mind this depends on whose commentary you read.) As Elijah ran, illusions of grandeur danced in his head: the death of state Baalism, a court chaplaincy, legislative prayer breakfasts, another opportunity to vindicate God's honor, and make His mark on the world. He is like many of us in the world today. We have visions of what God is going to do and we seem to be so disappointed when God does not live up to our expectations.

Here is Ahab who told Jezebel everything Elijah had done and how he had killed all the prophets with the sword. Jezebel sent a messenger to Elijah to say, "May the gods deal with me, be it ever so severely, if by this time tomorrow I do not make your life like that of one of them." Elijah was afraid and ran for his life. When he came to Beersheba in Judah, he left his servant there while he himself went a day's journey into the desert. He came to a broom tree, sat down under it and prayed that he might die. "I have had enough, LORD," he said. "Take my life; I am no better than my ancestors." Then he laid down under the tree and fell asleep (1 Kings 19:1-5).

Jezebel had another idea: "Dream on," she said and sent a messenger with this bit of terse verse: "May the gods deal with me, be it ever so severely, if by this time tomorrow I do not make your life like that of one of them" (19:2). Elijah's snappy rejoinder was to turn and flee: "Elijah was afraid and ran for his life" (19:3). The text may also be translated, "Elijah saw!" He got the picture! What happened to him has happened to many of us today.

Fueled by raw fear, Elijah ran all the way to Beersheba, a distance of about 100 miles., dropped from exhaustion and prayed that he might die. "I have had enough, Lord," he said. "Take my life; I am no better than my ancestors" (19:4). "Enough!" he cried. "I'm a failure! I quit!" Do you remember when you spend all your time and money on a project for the ministry, no one said thanks, or no one acknowledged it. We also could have been an object of someone's confusion, jealously, or mischief. The bottom line is things did not go our way, we were upset, confused and irritated and highly disappointed. So we ran!

This is what we see prophets do today in this generation. They come to a prophetic work, have success and on the out-set of not seeing full manifestation in a short time, they run away. What makes them run? For instance, just as Elijah "saw" the evil messenger, the contemporary prophet sees what they perceive as an evil messenger also. This messenger may remind them of past hurt. This messenger may remind them of unfilled promises. This messenger may awaken deep seeded unresolved feelings of confusion. This messenger will remind him of what's been buried alive.

One of the basic reasons prophets run today is that they sim-ply never let Jesus "plant" them so their roots can go down deep and bring forth fruit. The Bible suggests that without roots, we cannot flourish: "The righteous shall flourish like a palm tree, he shall grow like a cedar in Lebanon. Those who are planted shall flourish in the courts of our God" (Psalms 92:12-13).

God Himself established the prophetic order. As a prophet, you must develop within the root system that we refer to as pro-phetic companies, prophetic watering holes or prophetic minis-try to grow and flourish. There are prophets who just want to connect simply to be recognize. Then there are those who just want counsel, but they always seem to be on the fence of commitment or they always have a better way and will always look for a way out so they won't have to make any type of commitment; it is easier to run. The patterns of this prophet is similar to the wondering prophet who is always looking to be introduced to another circle as a prophet.

Prophetic leaders understand this clearly: when a prophet wants to connect only looking to get fed and comforted, but does not want to develop in the root system of commitment, it really is only a matter of time before they will run. They will always claim they have found the "greener grass" on the other side. Just as Elijah ran and hid and lied to God, the contemporary prophet of today will do the same thing to prophetic leadership. The shame is it's to the same leader, senior prophet or Apostle who they said God sent them to. Remember Elijah was in the will of God doing great miracles and then when his challenge came, he ran.

Prophets, even within the miracle there will be challenges. This is not the sign to run, but to cling to where God has you. You're running away is a sign of immaturity that must be dealt with for prophetic growth. Elijah's come-down was a classic case. He was over-extended and emotionally depleted, brooding over his feelings of inadequacy and apparent failure, he collapsed into self-pity, withdrawal, and self-destructive thoughts. Every one of us as prophets has times of deep discouragement. Time and pain will wear down our resolve. We are human. Elijah was broken in his spirit and bruised beyond repair. Prophets get weary of soul. The key is how we respond. Today's prophets many times, more often than not, choose to run and ignore. This is the place where they stop growing!

When we find no selfish pleasure, we have no time, and we have one excuse after the other. All of a sudden we start to rationalize like Elijah that it was not the will of God or ours to do his work. In the prophet's life, there is an abiding sense of failure. Our yoke seems unbearable. Our burdens are heavy beyond endurance. And what makes our difficulties even more grievous is that we feel such terrible loneliness: no one seems to care, no one shares our outlook, or even God seems to be shunning us. And so, like Elijah, we cry "Enough already!" This is classic for the prophet of today, as they say things like "my leader does not understand me," or "they have never been through this." Prophets, look at the fact that Elijah ran but he heard God, and Moses ran but he believed God. Whatever you run from is indicative of what you need to develop.

Communication with God to realize his plan in your life is critical. Today's prophet has the benefit of leadership, an Apostle or Senior Prophet, and yet the leadership suffers trying to evaluate why today's prophets run away, even after ordination in many cases. The dark moods of the prophet are nothing more than physical and emotional depletion. Like Elijah we've been running scared, overdoing everything, committing ourselves to more projects and plans than we could ever do. We string ourselves out, expending all our time and energy trying to be all things to all people at all times adding our will to God's, trying to do well what he never intended for us to do at all. In other words, we have an idea of what we want to do and we want Gods plan to fit into it for us and it will not! Then we start to feel guilty and worthless.

Prophets sometime will tax their bodies and give themselves no chance to recover. We provide no margins in which to adjust to unexpected emergencies. Overworked and under-slept, we finally reach our yield point and fold. Our bodies can't take it anymore. Unlike that battery-powered bunny, we just can't keep going. Prophets seem to forget that we're only human, that "we have this treasure [Christ's divinity] in vessels of common clay [our humanity]" (2 Corinthians 4:7). The treasure is the only enduring element; the rest of us is frail and gives way easily. "Fatigue makes cowards of us all," the great coach Vince Lombardi of the Green Bay Packers Football team said. It is so true. Look at Elijah; look at us.

We start to lose focus and lose our grasp on reality. We implode — withdraw into a state of self-condemnation and apathy. We lose focus and concentration. We say things that we would never say if we were fresh and well-rested. We make unwise decisions based on feelings of inadequacy, and sometimes the decisions are irreversible. We should never trivialize our weariness.

In other words, we come to leaders tired and unhealed and we refuse to heal. We hide it, we proclaim what God has said and we refuse to honor his word that we proclaim with our life. We are tired and when our "Challenge of Greatness" comes because we are unprepared prophets, we will run like Elijah. Unprepared prophets seem to always be reminded of their past and its failures, gossip of the day, and perception of what they think it should be. Just like Elijah, they run away. This is where Satan wants your mindset. So what does the prophet do? They run away.

Elijah lay down under the tree and fell asleep. All at once an angel touched him and said, "Get up and eat." He looked around, and there by his head was a cake of bread baked over hot coals and a jar of water. He ate and drank and then lay down again. The angel of the LORD came back a second time and touched him and said, "get up and eat, for the journey is too much for you." So he got up and ate and drank (1 Kings 19:5-8).

God understood Elijah's weary and despair, and he let him sleep. Sleep is God's gift to his weary servants: "He grants sleep to those he loves" (Psalm 127:2). Sometimes the most urgent and vital thing you can do is to take a complete rest. Being spiritual doesn't necessarily mean expending effort in ministry. It may mean eating supper and hitting the sack. If you don't get rest then you will be no good to anyone, and you will not be available to be at your best for God. Let's take away this excuse to run.

God sent his angel to touch Elijah. No lecture, no rebuke, no chiding, just a gentle touch from one of the Lord's tender angels waking Elijah to eat and drink. He commands his angels concerning us, to keep us in all our ways (Psalm 91:11). When will we learn that as contemporary prophets of today that we are not alone; we do have help.

Prophets, when you are running from Apostle to Apostle, ministry to ministry, from church to church, and you're wounded and hurt, that's when you need to be closest to God. Your situation may not be physical exhaustion like Elijah, but you may suffer from emotional exhaustion or any number of related symptoms. This is when God restores us, when we're down and out, when we have nothing left to give. He comes to take away our weariness. He never awakens anyone to disappointment, but to the good things love has prepared for us today. Somebody tell God thank you for his love of his prophets.

1 John 4:16 is a great example of this love. John, who learned God's love on Jesus' breast, tells in words so simple and direct: "We know and rely on the love God has for us." Prophets, we will go back to these words again and again in our prophetic journey. Perhaps the best way to know God's love is to experience it in times of disappointment and deep discouragement, when we feel most undeserving of it. "His loving kindness is better than life" (Psalm 63:3).

We now see the great Elijah who is strengthened by food and rest, the same Elijah who "traveled forty days and forty nights until he reached Horeb, the mountain of God. There he went into a cave and spent the night" (1 Kings19:9). In the strength of God's angel food, Elijah journeyed into the wilderness to Mount Horeb (Sinai), the mountain of revelation, where God always spoke his mind. There the Lord addressed the deeper elements of Elijah's discouragement. I challenge each prophet to read and reread those scriptures (1Kings 19). They are rich with revelation of God's love for us as his prophets.

Did you see that Elijah moved closer to God's plan for his life at the mountain? He was at his lowest point in his life, and he was getting the highest, most important revelation of his life. In other words he was in position to hear from God. Many time prophets of today run from ministry to ministry and never hear from God and fall into depression and out of ministry all together. We are missing revelation that we need.

Here is Elijah and the word of the Lord came to him: "What are you doing here, Elijah?" He replied, "I have been very zealous for the Lord God Almighty. The Israelites have rejected your covenant, broken down your altars, and put your prophets to death with the sword. I am the only one left, and now they are trying to kill me too." The Lord said, "Go out and stand on the mountain in the presence of the Lord, for the Lord is about to pass by." Then a great and powerful wind tore the mountains apart and shattered the rocks before the Lord, but the Lord was not in the wind. After the wind there was an earthquake, but the Lord was not in the earthquake. After the earthquake, came a fire, but the Lord was not in the fire. And after the fire came a gentle whisper. When Elijah heard it, he pulled his cloak over his face and went out and stood at the mouth of the cave. Then a voice said to him, "What are you doing here, Elijah?" (1Kings 19:9-13).

Elijah, like the prophet of today, can't answer the question clearly. Elijah starts to speak to God about his suffering and how he is the only one left. That was not true, and God told him. In other words, he had an excuse to justify his actions. Many have said that Elijah was simply confused. Even if you want to justify his actions, this is still not acceptable.

Prophets today will justify their actions based on perception much like Elijah. Question, prophet? How does God send you to an apostle, to a ministry or to a church to run away from with no divine word of departure? You just leave in dishonor. Then you tell and try to justify that it is the will of God? No, it's the will of an immature gift that does not want to mature.

You can't face your apostle or leaders so you leave with a note, text or email. The same person who you brought other prophets to, the same person or persons who you swore your allegiance to publicly, but you, the prophet, run away in the darkness and can't justify it without some excuse that makes no sense to you when asked. The sad thing is that many prophets like this never bring the issue to leadership. They left without honor just as Elijah did, or they went to leadership and got an answer they did not want and now the old familiar line of "God told me" became the standard excuse of your departure. This is how Satan destroys prophets through prophetic relationships within prophetic operations that are not stable. Leaders, we must work to stabilize our relationships and our operations for the work of the gospel.

Look at Elijah. The only evidence of God was a still, small voice; a nearly inaudible whisper. You never know about God. Prophets hear this, God may appear in extraordinary and melodramatic ways such as a hurricane, earthquake, or storm. But God's usually much less obvious to us. God's heroics, when they appear, are rarely as expected. He works in quietness. His Spirit gently moves like the wind, here and there, touching one, touching another, and working in silence to get his work done. The obvious is usually not seen; God's best efforts are rarely seen.

This is what every prophet needs to understand. Just because you as a prophet don't see this or you don't see that, you run from ministry to ministry. Part of you not seeing is part of your test to build you as a Prophet of God. Faith that can't be tested is faith that can't be trusted. Prophets who run, retreat and go into self-justification never pass this test and seem to wonder from place to place.

Elijah, as great as he was, had unrealistic expectations of God from his perspective. If you're a prophet, you have had to deal with this also. He had seen the Lord manifest himself in stupendous display on Mount Carmel. He expected a repeat performance: that God would make short work of Jezebel, blasting her off the face of the earth. No doubt he wanted to see it also, but what he got was the scare of his life and he ran. Elijah had a contract on his life and total exhaustion that were coupled with disappointment and depression.

Today's prophets expect certain things to happen just because they do the work of God. We have a right to expect Gods best, but we also need to realize God will use our circumstances of life to qualify us for the next season, the season of prophetic elevation. Prophets we seem to do well for a season until that "mantle challenge" happens and then we feel like Elijah and run away. Like Elijah we blame the world instead of blaming the person we see in the mirror.

Prophets, your ministry is developed by working with other prophets and special God sent people, and not by waddling in your hurt and never putting down any spiritual roots. Elisha had to become part of Elijah's vision for a season. Timothy had to become part of Paul's vision for a season. When someone becomes part of someone else's vision, it causes them to be connected and to grow in the things of God. This is the gift of prophetic empowerment. Both Elisha and Timothy needed to be connected before they could be released for their ministry. They did not leave prematurely. In Elisha's case, if he had left too soon, he would never have received the double anointing.

Elisha benefited because God's way of correcting Elijah's perspective was to bring him to the place of revelation, which is what he must do with us again and again. It's in that quiet place that we hear God's voice. That's where we hear the truth, the whole truth and nothing but the truth. That's where we get real. This is the place that most prophets do not know exists in their lives.

Ever wonder why some prophets feel that no one should get any disease, no one dies from cancer, no one fails in marriage, or no one falls to mental illness. Everyone lives happily ever after. But that's not the way it is. Life is difficult. The world is painful in any case, but it is quite unbearable if anybody gives us the idea that we are meant to like it. When people say that life is hard, you will know from deposited experience. You as a Prophet will find that answer more satisfying than anything else. Every new season and every new assignment will confirm that life is difficult and demanding. This is the price of the prophetic anointing; any other response is unrealistic.

Life will rarely go as we think it should. You should not to worry. Things we call tragedies, setbacks, and failures are opportunities for God. He knows how to draw glory even from our greatest ruin. Not to be downcast after failure is one of the marks of true sanctity. The hour of deepest humiliation, when we feel defective and utterly disqualified, may be the hour that God wants to use us the greatest in unparalleled ways. Years of what we view as "wasted" effort may be the years when God plants an eternal harvest.

Let's explore what happens when prophets run away. Let's continue to look at Elijah as our example. He was afraid (1 King 19:3). He knew that this was no idle threat (1 Kings 18:4 and 13). Prophets of today are afraid of any number of issues such as acceptance and possible persecution, just to name a few. Think about it as you look at 1 Kings 18 verses 4 and 13. One day he had stood fearless on Mount Carmel and now he trembled at the threat of Jezebel. Can this be attributed, in part, to his physical exhaustion? James 5:17 states, "Elijah was a man with a nature like ours." We should strive to see our similarities with God's great biblical Prophets.

First Kings 19:3. Elijah ran from Jezreel to Beersheba, a debatable distance in excess of 100 miles. Beersheba was in the southern part of the kingdom of Judah, out of Ahab and

Jezebel᾽s jurisdiction. Prophets of today will try to get as far away from what they are running. Notice that he also left his servant in Beersheba (1 Kings 19:3). This was the same servant mentioned in 1 Kings 18:43 who kept watch for the rain cloud while Elijah prayed. The prophet of today will leave their apostle, brother/sister prophets, and everything to achieve a goal that is so sudden and so important that it does not warrant a proper exit. This is why we get into trouble by speaking ill of God's leaders. Speaking about a leader when you are uneducated on their situation, especially of a personal nature, is not acceptable or appropriate for a prophet.

Elijah had an opportunity to spend some time alone with God. There he was, a day's journey into the wilderness sitting under a juniper tree (1 Kings 19:4). The prophet of today will run away, leave, go spin their wheels and proclaim all is well and seek like-minded confused prophets to justify their joint hurts instead of going to God.

Elijah asked God to let him die (1 Kings 19:4). "I've had enough. Take away my life. I've got to die sometime, and it might as well be now." The prophet of today says the Lord is sending them in a different direction, but they can't seem to announce it to whom honor is due. Instead the feel that they might as well run and hide. How many of us are guilty of this type of behavior?

God will confront people with their sin, either through His Word or through His servants, in this case the prophets. As long as God's prophet was around, Jezebel could not carry out all the evil she wanted to do. In her anger, she vowed to kill him.

Sometimes people are angry or irritated with prophets because they are a reminder of their sin and evil practices. Prophets run based on factors that they determine are unspoken and overwhelming situations like Elijah. Prophet, you may think if you could just get away from God's people, everything would be okay. Yet, we can never run from God. He loves you too much.

CHAPTER FIVE

Voices That A Prophet Hears

"Who Are You Listening To?"

All of us at some time or another have heard people say that they were "called" to be a prophet or "called" to the mission field or another five-fold ministry gift. Often what they mean is that they felt a strong desire or burden in that direction. They prayed about it and received several confirmations that this was what the Lord wanted them to do. The Bible tells us that we need to be led by the Holy Spirit. Therefore, it must be possible for every one of us to discern the promptings and guidance of the Holy Spirit within us! As a Prophet you must hear the voice of God. This lesson is not about all the different ways in which God speaks to us, such as dreams, visions, tongues and interpretation, prophecies, and so on, but as a prophet practical guidance is needed on how to discern God's voice

Four Voices A Prophet Will Hear

1.　　Prophets, the voice that is perhaps the most obvious is our own voice. In addition to our speaking voice, we also talk to ourselves inside our heads, we see images and pictures inside our heads. We have emotions, feelings, desires, and so on. Our minds tell us what we think, our wills tell us what we want, and our emotions tell us how we feel. The Bible refers to our minds, wills, and emotions as our "flesh nature." How many of us are listening to our flesh nature and are willing to admit it has affected our walk with God. Prophet, this is the one voice you must know and not allow it to rule you.

2.　　We also hear the voice of other people. Sometimes people say things which are true, noble, and good, and sometimes people say things which are just the opposite. What are you hearing from the voice of other people? We see too many modern generation prophets swayed by the voice of other people. Many times God will put a voice in your life just as he did Elisha; Elisha listened to Elijah and we see how he turned out (1 Kings 19).

3.　　The third voice we hear is of the devil. The devil has crafty ways of speaking to us, which he has perfected. He is subtle. What he does is to throw thoughts into our minds like flaming arrows, and he speaks to us through the worldly ideas and viewpoints that he has injected into other people. As Prophets we must extinguish all the flaming arrows of the evil one (Ephesians 6:16).

4.   The most important voice is the most subtle. It is the voice of God. God does not speak to us in our minds. He speaks to us in our spirits because that is where the Holy Spirit lives. Most of us as prophets tend to spend most of our thought life in our heads, in other words in "the mind of the flesh" (Romans 8:7,), focused on the sensory world around us where our physical senses and our thoughts, feelings, desires, and emotions are constantly being bombarded and stimulated in worldly, carnal, fleshly ways.

As Prophets we tend to live on the shallow surface, so to speak. We rarely venture deeper where the Spirit of God lives within us. Many of us do not know where our spirits are nor how to hear and be led by our spirits. Because of this, we leave ourselves wide open to fall for the many deceptions of the devil. Prophets we must learn how to be more Spirit-led.

The Prophets Greatest Enemy

Who is our greatest enemy? If you said the devil... wrong! The prophet's greatest enemy is the prophet's mind, will, and emotions, which the Bible sometimes refers to as our "sin nature" or our "flesh." Prophet, if we did not have a sinful flesh nature, then the devil would have no hold on us. Jesus had a body made of flesh and blood, but He did not have a sinful flesh nature as we do. Therefore the devil had no hold on Him (John 14:30).

First Thessalonians 5:23 says that we are made up of "spirit, soul and body." Your body is aware of the physical world around you, your spirit is aware of God within you, and everything else is your soul, which is aware of "self." Your soul is made up of your mind (what you think), your will (what you want), and your emotions (what you feel). Our spirits were "regenerated" (made alive) the moment we were saved (John 3:3-8), and our bodies will be made immortal when Jesus returns for us (1 Corinthians 15:51-53), but we must wage a daily battle against our "flesh nature." You see, the problem is that our "flesh" is ungodly. It is our sin nature, and that's why the Bible tells us to "crucify" our flesh.

How Does A Prophet Recognize God's Voice?

In order to hear God's voice and to discern His leading for your daily life, don't expect God to speak to you in a sensational, spectacular, supernatural way. Prophets have a natural tendency to want God to speak out loud to us in some obvious way so that we know that it was Him and so that we know what we are supposed to do. God occasionally does speak to people in the audible voice of God or in some other sensational way, but those are not His usual ways of speaking to us. Why? Because faith is God's way, and without faith it is impossible to please

Him (Hebrews 11:6). The thing about faith is that it requires that we don't have all of our questions answered!

We must realize, that if God were to speak out loud to us all the time just so we'd know it is He who is speaking to us, then we don't need faith to hear him. On the other hand, if God speaks so softly to us that we need to get into the habit of listening closely to our spirits and drawing closer to God in order to hear Him better, then there is a lot of faith involved. It requires cultivating a deeper, more personal, more intimate relationship with the Lord. This is exactly what God is after with each and every prophet! Once a Prophet gets past the "hang up" of needing to hear from God in spectacular, loud, supernatural ways, then the prophet will find themselves beginning to recognize the still, quiet voice of God. The Holy Spirit lives in your spirit, which is sometimes called your "heart" (2 Corinthians 1:22) or your "inner man" (Romans 7:22), and that is where you will usually hear Him speaking to you, prophet.

There are some major differences in the way that God speaks to us compared with the way that the devil speaks to us. The devil shoots condemning thoughts into our minds, but the Spirit always builds us up. The Holy Spirit will convict prophets of sin in our lives, but He never brings condemnation. We as Prophets need to learn to discern the difference between the two.

Conviction makes us aware of our actions that were sinful and that need to be confessed and repented of, but condemnation makes us feel that we are bad or worthless. Prophets, self-pity and self-condemnation comes from the devil, so always resist these impulses and don't allow yourself to give in to them. The Holy Spirit always speaks in line with the Word of God, and this is why it is so important to get to know the Word of God, which is the will of God. The Apostle John said that the Word was with God and the Word was God, and then the Word became flesh and dwelt with us (John 1:1, 14). God and His Word cannot be separated.

The Holy Spirit illuminates the right Scripture at the right time. Sometimes the Holy Spirit will bring a Scripture verse up within you, just the right verse to meet your needs at that moment when God is using you. Prophets, you also need to realize the Holy Spirit won't be able to help you in this way if you rarely read your Bible and you don't have the Scripture verses down inside of you to begin with! The Bible says that "the Word of God is living and active" (Hebrews 4:12), but Scripture needs to be living in you in order for it to be active in your life.

Prophets, we must be obedient in the small things, the everyday things which God might prompt you to do or not to do, and as you develop the habit of instantly obeying these things (whether your flesh wants to or not) then you will find that your sensitivity and discernment will begin to increase. Keep in mind that God always has your best interests at heart, so He will never tell you to do something or to quit doing something unless it is for your benefit and helps you to come up higher in the things of God.

God cannot trust you to operate in His supernatural power with any great degree of authority if you are full of yourself, always talking about yourself, boasting or bragging about yourself, or if you are a prophet who likes to judge, criticize and gossip about other people, especially prophets. The gifts of the Spirit operate by faith, and faith operates by love - love for God and love for others, not love for yourself (Galatians 5:6)!

Many prophets have not been taught how to operate in the supernatural gifts of the Spirit which God has made available to them. They have not been taught how to hear God in their spirits and have not been adequately taught that they need to constantly crucify their flesh. Is it any wonder that most prophets never see the supernatural power of God in their daily lives?

Begin obeying the small, subtle signals that the Holy Spirit gives you, and your sensitivity will increase by leaps and bounds. Prophets, you will be wrong sometimes, but don't be afraid to make mistakes. God often prefers to teach us through the school of life, not through giving us instantaneous supernatural knowledge of all things. Don't hesitate to admit it when you thought you had heard from God but it turned out that you were wrong. Be honest with yourself, be humble and transparent with your leaders. Be faithful with God.

Prophets, learn that before you make any type of major decision (especially if it is something that you thought of all by yourself without any promptings from God), ask the Lord to give you some type of confirmation that this is His will. God's ways are higher than our ways. Also keep in mind that when God speaks to you, it will not always make sense to your brain.

One time Jesus told Peter to go out into the deep and let down his nets for a haul. Peter replied, "Master, we've worked hard all night and haven't caught anything. But because you say so, I will let down the nets" (Luke 5:5). Even though it didn't make sense to Peter's brain, he obeyed the Lord and proceeded to get a miracle. You will only see miracles by obeying God rather than obeying your brain or your feelings. Remember, your mind, your will and your feelings do not get a vote! Prophet, when you learn this you will grow by leaps and bounds.

Prophet, your job is to be obedient to what God tells you to do, both in His written Word and His spoken Word. We should always wait on His timing as He works everything out in His perfect, individual plan for your life. The only way a prophet can mature in Christ is by developing the fruit of the Spirit, and one of these fruits is patience (Galatians 5:22-23).

Another way that the Holy Spirit guides prophets is by putting strong desires into our hearts. When God wants us to do something, sometimes He gives us the desire to do it. It is then the prophet's job to ask Him to bring it to pass and then to wait patiently (sometimes for years) until He places us in that new thing which is the desire of our heart. Prophets, make sure that you are following God's desires and not your own desires. This can be tricky sometimes, and it requires putting our own desires and reasoning completely into neutral, wanting God's desires above all else. It is much easier to discern God's desires when we want one thing but we feel that God desires just the opposite.

Things A Prophet Can Do To Hear God Better

Prophets, you must develop your inner discernment and be able to hear the voice of God more clearly and accurately. In your prayer life, ask God to help you hear His voice and discern His daily leading in your life. In order to hear God better, we need to get to know God better. When we think we have heard something from God, we should make sure that what we heard is in line with the Word of God, which means that we need to know what the Word of God says.

Make sure that the Bible version you are using is easy for you to read, otherwise you will become discouraged very quickly. Ask God where you should start reading in the Bible. Remember that your goal is quality and not quantity. Instead, your goal should be to feed on the Word of God, which is "bread" for your spirit, and to allow the Holy Spirit to illuminate the deeper spiritual truths of His Word to you so that you can get to know God better.

Prophets, if you are not spiritually discerning what His Book says (1 Corinthians 2:13-14), then you are just reading words on a page which are doing you very little good. "Head knowledge" will not get you very far. What you need is revelation from the Holy Spirit as you read God's Word. Read His Book with the goal of getting to know Him and His character, and to learn what you can do to honor Him with your life.

Prophet, the Bible was not just written for people "back then," it was written to you. Therefore, try "personalizing" the Bible as you read it so that you can get the full impact of what God is saying to you. "I tell you the truth, anyone who has faith in me will do what I have been doing. He will do even greater things than these because I am going to the Father. And I will do whatever you ask in my name, so that the Son may bring glory to the Father. You may ask me for anything in my name, and I will do it. If you love me, you will obey what I command (John 14:12-15).

Prophet, here's how it sounds to you personally: I tell you the truth Ken, if you have faith in me, son you will do what I have been doing. Ken, you will do even greater things than these, because I am going to the Father. Ken, know that I will do whatever you ask in my name, so that the Son may bring glory to the Father. Ken, you may ask me for anything in my name, and I will do it. Ken, my son, If you love me, you will obey what I command." Prophets, this is from John 14:12-15 and it's personal. Now use your name and see how personal it gets quickly. See what a difference it makes when we "personalize" the Bible? It makes it easy to see that Jesus is speaking directly to us through His Word!

He said to them, "Go into all the world and preach the good news to all creation. Whoever believes and is baptized will be saved, but whoever does not believe will be condemned. And

these signs will accompany those who believe: In my name
they will drive out demons; they will speak in new tongues; they
will pick up snakes with their hands; and when they drink deadly poison, it will not hurt them at all; they will place their hands
on sick people, and they will get well" (Mark 16:15-18).

During your time alone with the Lord, stop expecting to feel
something special. We are told to live by faith (2 Corinthians
5:7), not run our lives by our feelings. There are times when a
real joy may bubble and a "Holy Laughter" comes. Then there
are times when you may weep. There are times when you may
feel a special closeness to the Lord. Often you may not feel anything at all. Prophet, trust that the Lord knows what's best for
you, and if it feels like He's not even in the same room with you,
then just trust that He is trying to draw you closer with a "dry
time," or He is trying to stretch my faith during the "dry times."
This is so true, especially for a prophet.

Prophet, just trust that He is with you and He hears you, and
don't base anything on experiences and feelings. Prophet, you
may lay hands on someone who had cancer, but they didn't "feel"
any different. However, when they went to the doctor, they discovered that there was not a trace of cancer. This person may
be healed of cancer even though they didn't feel anything, and
Prophet, God is at work in you even when you don't feel anything. Just trust Him.

Your spirit wants to be close to God and to fellowship with
Him, but your flesh wants to fight you all the way, and the devil
really wants to fight you on this! Just keep coming back day

after day and spending regular time with the Lord. Because you are honoring Him and He is pleased with your faith and your sacrifice, ultimately He will reward you.

Prophet, sometimes you will need to wait for a while and keep expecting and watching for the answer in whatever manner that God chooses to speak to you. For example, you might pray,

"Lord, teach me how to be more patient." Instead of giving you an immediate answer to your prayer, you might find that suddenly you are getting caught in more traffic jams, you start getting all the slowest lines at the grocery store, or maybe some aggravating people will begin to come into your life. This is God speaking to you, answering your prayer by giving you opportunities to kill off that impatient flesh of yours!

Prophets, sometimes God will bring frustrating circumstances and people into our lives to act as "sandpaper" against our flesh in order to smooth out the rough spots in us, and our job is to maintain a good attitude and to kill off those things that flare up in our flesh (anger, impatience, pride, and so on). As we cooperate with the sanctifying work of the Holy Spirit and grow in spiritual maturity, we will find ourselves hearing God more clearly and accurately on how to grow by leaps and bounds in spiritual maturity

Habakkuk 2 says to write the vision, what you hear from God, because you will be surprised at how quickly you'll forget what He "said." You will be surprised at how quickly you'll convince yourself that it wasn't really God speaking after all. When you receive a flash of discernment within you, know that it was

God. However, the next day you might not be so certain that it was God, so consider writing it down while you still have that "knowing" within you. Also, when you have trained yourself to hear God's voice, you will sometimes hear Him tell you things which will happen in your life in the future. This is why it is a good idea to write down the date when you hear things from God, then you can look back and read those prophecies that are now coming to pass.

For example, the apostle Paul heard from God better than almost anyone who ever lived, and it is no coincidence that he also spoke in tongues more than anyone else (1 Corinthians 14:18). Paul said that we "edify" ourselves when we speak in tongues ("He who speaks in a tongue edifies himself" (1 Corinthians 14)), which means that it encourages us, benefits us, strengthens and builds up our inner faith, and improves us spiritually. The book of Jude also says that we can build ourselves up by praying in the Spirit: "But you, beloved, build yourselves up [founded] on your most holy faith - make progress, rise like an edifice higher and higher - praying in the Holy Spirit" (Jude 1:20). Praying in the Spirit is much more important than most of us realize.

The apostle Paul spoke about our consciences quite frequently. He often said that he kept a good conscience or a clear conscience before God (Acts 23:1, 24:16, 1 Corinthians 4:4, 2 Timothy 1:3). He said that we should do the same (Romans 13:5, 1 Timothy 1:5, 19, 3:9) so that we don't shipwreck our faith. Notice that Paul could tell that he was hearing from God by listening to his conscience: "I speak the truth in Christ, I am not lying, my conscience confirms it in the Holy Spirit" (Romans

9:1). "Now this is our boast: Our conscience testifies that we have conducted ourselves in the world, and especially in our relations with you, in the holiness and sincerity that are from God" (2 Corinthians 1:12). Paul also said that our consciences "bear witness" to the truth (Romans 2:15), that the truth is "plain to your conscience" (2 Corinthians 5:11), and that "The Spirit himself testifies with our spirit" (Romans 8:16) to confirm the truth. Learn to obey every twinge of your conscience and let peace be your umpire continually.

Luke 9:23 "And He said to all, If any person wills to come after Me, let him deny himself [disown himself, forget, lose sight of himself and his own interests, refuse and give up himself] and take up his cross daily and follow Me [cleave steadfastly to Me, conform wholly to My example in living and, if need be, in dying, also]." This is what happened to Moses. He understood that his mind of the flesh (with its carnal thoughts and purposes) was hostile to God, for it could not submit itself to God's Law; indeed it cannot.

Prophets who are living the life of the flesh, catering to the appetites and impulses of their carnal nature, cannot please or satisfy God, or be acceptable to Him (Romans 8:7- 8). The apostle Paul said that the mind of the flesh has carnal, worldly, sinful thoughts and purposes, and that it is hostile to God and cannot submit to God! Paul went on to say that if we are living according to our "flesh nature" then we cannot please God. "The Lord knows the thoughts and reasoning's of the [humanly] wise and recognizes how futile they are" (1 Corinthians 3:20).

The apostle Paul tells us that our "flesh" is our Godless human nature, and that our natural desires are opposed to the things of the Spirit and are continually in conflict with the Spirit. The solution, Paul says, is to walk and live habitually in the Spirit, always being responsive to and controlled by and guided by the Spirit within us. Prophets, when we are busy analyzing things in our minds and trying to figure out the solutions to our problems and so on, it hinders us from hearing from The Lord. May God bless you as you learn how to hear and obey His voice within you!

CHAPTER SIX

Unhealthy Friends In A Prophets Life

"Who Is In Your Life Talking To You?"

One of the prophet's greatest test is what we learn from life experiences with so-called friends, associates and brothers and sister prophets. From them we learn how to pray for those we love, or are in covenant with. Let's look at Job's life to learn more about this process. While we look at Job and don't necessarily consider him a prophet, there is a lot prophets can learn from studying Job. Job has prophet-like situations. Job's friends are an example of what not to do when friends are suffering.

Job is the righteous man God spoke about to Satan. God identified Job as his servant. As a prophet you are a servant of God.
God gave Satan license to afflict Job. Job lost his possessions and
his health. His seven sons and three daughters, for whom he had
interceded daily, pleading their cases before God as a defense
attorney might plead their cases in court, were killed in a freak-
ish windstorm (Job 1:18-19). Job lost much for the cause of God.

Prophet, how much are you willing to lose for the cause of
God? Job did lose everything to include his health. The question is do we as prophets realize that we have to lose something
to facilitate the growing process? We see this in the life of Job.

As a prophet, some of your greatest loses will be on a personal
level. For Job, on a personal level, he lost his children. His wife
lost her confidence in the Lord and any respect she had for her
husband. She eventually encouraged him to forget his integrity,
to "curse God and die" (Job 2:9). This will happen in the lives of
some prophets. People in your life who have spent time with you
in your suffering as you grow prophetically know how hard it is
to remain present without trying to give you answers. It is many
times excruciating for a friend to suffer silently with a prophet
who must rebuild his or her life piece by piece, without any certainty about the outcome. Friends will want to investigate what
went wrong and identify a solution. We would rather give a
reason for the suffering be it right, be it wrong, than to accept
the mystery at the heart of suffering could very well be the will
of God. Job's friends succumb to this temptation. As a prophet
rest assured you will have friend who will also. How much harm
have well-intentioned people caused by giving pious-sounding

answers to suffering, especially in the life of a prophet. Job's friends can't lament with Job or even acknowledge that they lack a basis for judging him. They are hell-bent (literally, given Satan's role) on defending God by placing the blame on Job. This is why prophets are so unable to connect with prophets. Because as friends' speeches continue, their rhetoric becomes increasingly hostile. Faced with the self-imposed choice of blaming Job or blaming God, they harden their hearts against their former friend. Prophets, when you suffer or are going through, you must realize this, it is really part of your process as it was with Job.

Another great loss for Job was the loss of relationships with his friends. Job's friends became a burden rather than a blessing. Those who should have been sensitive to his needs and supportive in their actions during his time of trial only added to his burden. Interestingly, each of them represents a type of friend no one wants when going through trial.

Prophets, listen closely. As we look at the friends of Job, perhaps in them we will learn the behaviors to avoid when our friends are suffering trials and also when we are going through things ourselves. We can develop an earnest desire to become effective prayer advocates when others have walked away. The Law of Reciprocity says we will get what we give.

When Job needed loving, practical friends to assist and support him in his hour of need, his friend Eliphaz decided to be "super-spiritual" instead. He took it upon himself to bring correction to Job: "Job, I know you're in a lot of pain right now, but I'd like to have a word with you. You've offered counsel and encouragement to lots of troubled people in the past. And you've been the first to support those who have stumbled. But now it's obvious you discouraged regarding the trouble that has come to you. I know you think you're a righteous man, but let me ask you a question: when have you ever heard of an innocent man being destroyed?" (Job 4:2-7) "There is no end to your iniquities," says Eliphaz in Job 22:5, and then he invents some iniquities to charge against Job. "You have given no water to the weary to drink, and you have withheld bread from the hungry" (Job 22:8). "You have sent widows away empty-handed, and the arms of the orphans you have crushed" (Job 22:9).

Eliphaz was out of touch with the reality of Job's intense suffering. The unsettling truth about friends who manifest the "I can hear God better than you" syndrome is that many of them have never personally experienced a genuine breaking from God. They're calling may be totally different from yours and they can't see or understand what you are dealing with. People with a religious spirit speak out of their soullessness and not from true brokenness.

Job is hurting. He didn't need religion. He needed relationship. He needed a listening ear, not a sermon. Job needed an intercessor, not an instructor. Eliphaz thought he was serving God when in fact he was an unknowing pawn of Satan. When called to the witness stand in the gap for Job, he became a star witness for Satan instead. Prophet, when we are suffering, may God deliver us from our religious friends. Prophet, decide right now that when your friends are suffering, you will relate to them with compassion and empathy.

An idealist is defined as one who adheres to philosophical theories of perfection and excellence and concepts of flawless morality. This may sound good, but real life isn't quite this pristine. When suffering life's trials, we need neither religious, holier-than-thou friends to scold us nor idealistic prophetic friends to rebuke us. Hearing Job's explanation, idealist friend Bildad replied: "Job, what you are saying about your situation is nothing but 'hot air.' God doesn't pervert justice. You know your children died because of their sin. So, I think it's high time that you plead with God for your own life. If you are the righteous man you think you are, He will restore your health and other losses. Scripture says that God won't reject the righteous or bless the wicked" (Job 8:1-7).

Many five-fold ministry gifts, especially the prophets of today, have overlooked the powerful process of suffering and trials that God has designed to produce godliness in each of our lives. Let's not forget that Timothy says, "All that will live godly in Christ Jesus shall suffer persecution" (2 Tim. 3:12). Why doesn't the prophet of today recognize this? We like to say we are over whelmed with our life, many times with the same responsibilities that our peers have, and we want to be recognized on the same level as our peers who pay the price for God.

Prophets, if you never go through the process, or overlook the process, when suffering befalls a friend or especially another prophet, we are apt to assume it is God's judgment for sin of that prophet. When trouble befalls us, we are apt to be totally confused because we don't see the benefit of suffering for the anointing (1 Pet. 1:7-9; 2 Pet. 1:3-10; 2:9; James 1:2-4) for the purpose of suffering.

Sometimes God, for His own reasons, will allow an idealistic friend to add to our test. At times we all need false and idealistic concepts to be broken. Perhaps through an idealistic friend we can see our blindness and resolve to fully surrender our hearts to God (Psalm 51:17). Please understand that these "holier than thou" friends sometimes allow us to see ourselves.

A person who lives a life of legalism adheres to a literal and excessively religious moral code. The New Testament Pharisees were the legalists of their day. They monitored themselves and others by the Levitical law. Yet Jesus reprimanded them for neglecting "the more important matters of the law—justice, mercy and faithfulness (Matt. 23:23, NIV)."

No doubt the whole spirit of their religion was summed up in self-righteousness, not in confession of sin or humility. This was the kind of friend Job had in Zophar, the legalist! Zophar said: "How I wish God would tell you the truth about your situation, Job! He knows deceitful and evil men when He sees them. If you repent and put away your sin, then God will re- move your shame" (Job 11:4-6,11,13-15). With friends like this, who needs enemies? Apparently there was no one to plead the case for Job. His wife and friends all were against him. Does this sound like you prophet?

Let's not allow ourselves to become "Job's friends." When your friends are going through trials, do not be a religious Eliphaz, an idealistic Bildad or a legalistic, know-it-all Zophar who is out of touch with his own pain. Let's agree to be spiritual defense attorneys who come alongside to bring carefully prayed-over and gently presented Godly counsel, loving support and encouragement.

Sooner or later you become a defender. When God finished the work He was doing in Job, He promoted him from the role of suffering to be the exponent of his double portion anointing. "After the Lord had said these things to Job, he said to Eliphaz the Temanite, 'I am angry with you and your two friends, because you have not spoken of Me what is right, as my servant Job has" (Job 42:7). What a turnaround! See how Job let God fight his battle. Job's friends had failed to defend him in his trial. They had criticized, mocked and accused him. His friends had not understood the process of trial. Under Satan's spells they inadvertently served as strong witnesses. In so doing, they had even falsely accused God. Now God's judgment weighed heavily upon them. Judge Jehovah was about to pass sentence on them.

Then our merciful Judge gave Job's friends these surprising instructions: "So now take seven bulls and seven rams and go to my servant Job and sacrifice a burnt offering for yourselves. My servant Job will pray for you, and I will accept his prayer and not deal with you according to your folly. You have not spoken of Me what is right as my servant Job has" (Job 42:8). When God sends these people to you do the right thing, pray for them. Eliphaz the Temanite, Bildad the Shuhite and Zophar the

Naamathite did what the Lord told them; and the Lord accepted Job's prayer (Job 42v. 9).

Wow! The Judge sent Eliphaz, Bildad and Zophar God back to Job! As their spiritual attorney, Job was to plead their cases in prayer. And Job was no novice! Having defended his children and stood trial himself, Job the intercessor would not be praying detached, unfeeling, lifeless, ineffective prayers. As a Prophet learn these lessons as you are called on to stand in the gap for your friends who betray you! Every Prophet needs to understand what Job understood:

1.   He understood the pain and agony someone experiences when standing trial.

2.   He knew the fear, loneliness and severity of facing trial without a Godly support team.

3.   He would represent his friends well before the Judge of heaven.

Prophets, the trials you have suffered, when understood in the context of God's overall purposes and properly applied, can be used to a kingdom advantage as you intercede for others who are standing trial today. For Job's friends, the best part was that their victory was guaranteed before their case even came to trial! God said to Job's wayward friends, "I will accept his [Job's] prayer and not deal with you according to your folly."

Job passes the pest, and Prophet you must pass the test. As long as Job remained the self-absorbed defendant, primarily concerned with his own need, he was a victim. It was only when he became a God-conscious, God-ordained, anointed defender of others that he experienced his own victory! "And the Lord turned the captivity of Job, when he prayed for his friends" (Job 42:10). This is growth Prophet!

Yes, Job's captivity was turned when he prayed for his friends. When Job focused on God and others, his own captivity was turned! This is what Jesus taught us to do when He gave us the two greatest commandments: "'Love the Lord your God with all your heart and with all your soul and with all your mind and with all your strength...Love your neighbor as yourself'" Mark 12:30-31. Prophet, are you currently enrolled in "the school of suffering?" Perhaps you have been experiencing some Job-like trials of your own. When will they end? That's really the wrong question. The question we should ask is, "What will they produce?" And that, Prophet, is largely up to you. If you are facing an issue, look for another person who needs a good defense attorney and become that person's advocate before the throne of God in prayer.

It could be that your captivity, like Job's, will be turned as you pray for your friends and others! Immerse yourself in their victory, and you will likely discover your own! "So the Lord blessed the latter end of Job more than his beginning" (Job 42:12). May this also be said of you! Consider and seek friends who will celebrate with you, respect you and honor who you are in God. Do not try to hold on to unfruitful relationships that will only drain you and never empower you!

Nicknames for friends will vary, but we all have or had unhealthy type friends that ranged from   dictator, authoritarian and control freak to back stabber. Prophets, these monster type friends have little regard for the anointed relationships of God for that matter. Instead, their first priority is self, masked by other agendas. These type friends may use pressure tactics, political maneuvering, and/or persuasive speech in order to manipulate a situation into their behalf. Watch these type friends. When they don't get their way, they will:

1. Move on to others fast,
2. Cause a stir in their current relationships, and
3. Blame others for not following in their drama.

As a general rule, unhealthy friends may have some combination of the following traits:

1. Are always right and never wrong and wants to be the center of everything
2. Cannot accept criticism without becoming defensive.
3. Are not willing to share the opportunities.
4. Do not support other prophets or anyone's ministries but theirs.
5. Overly use the personal pronoun "I."
6. Resist accountability or will not develop a strong solid relationship with a leader.
7. Feels threatened by other gifted prophets or five-fold ministry gifts.
8. Will always surround themselves with "yes men" rather than edifying leaders.

9. Do not entrust or respect other gifted ministry to other leaders.

10. Will always undermine programs/ministries that they cannot control.

CHAPTER SEVEN

Developing The Inner Life Of The Prophet

"The Answer Is On The Inside"

There is a difference between Moses and almost all the prophets who followed him. Moses was familiar with God's plan and saw each prophetic assignment within the context of that plan. Today as prophets, we struggle to understand the details of what God's plan is. Today's Prophets seem to almost always attempt to deduce the wider implications of the master plan. Moses understood details we don't seem to in this day and time.

Why was Moses accorded the distinction as the greatest and most special prophet of God? Let's look at his life because it starts with his inner man and what he does. Moses was the most humble man on earth and Moses did not view himself as a separate entity from God. He was completely detached from himself with no sense of independent ego. His entire consciousness was absorbed within God.

In Exodus 25 God shows us a picture of our journey towards this "more excellent way" when we observe the Tabernacle of Moses. This was the tabernacle that was built in the wilderness after God delivered His people from Egypt. Let's look as we journey into the tabernacle as prophets of God.

We have accepted Jesus Christ into our heart and decided to follow Him. Picture this, we now have found ourselves in the tabernacle of God, we are in Christ. We see white walls that represented the "Righteousness of God in Christ" surrounding the tabernacle. We are the righteousness in Christ Jesus as the New Testament declare. Whether you act like it or not does not change this fact. Following the "more excellent way" of God will cause you to walk in this fact.

Why is it a reality that it is difficult to walk in? Thanks for asking! The reason is that our inner man (spirit man) became righteous by faith in Jesus even though the soul man was still quite the same as the day before. The soul man still knew little of God's way, of God's mind and how to yield to that which is within. Christ made his home in our heart, yet there are many areas of that home we have not allowed Him into, let alone allowed Him to become master of those areas.

Prophets understand that The Tabernacle is composed of the Outer Court, the Inner Court (also called the Holy Place), and the Most Holy Place (also called the Holy of Holies). The Holy Place and the Holy of Holies are both covered under the same tent which is called the Tent of Testimony or Tent of the Congregation. This symbolizes those who abide in the Inner Courts of God who will become a true testimony with true unity in brotherly love. This is what Moses did with his life. He gave God everything, literally everything. Inside this TENT is where God wants every part of your life! The lesson here is that as prophets we must give God everything like Moses did.

As a Prophet, you must examine your life. There can't remain one area that stays undealt with, for God's word goes forth to bring all areas into subjection. Every area of your life must become a testimony. Every area of your life must reflect the unity we have with walking with God in His garden, in a relationship that we have chosen even though we were tempted to choose the things that separate us from relationship. This is our real life reality as we process into maturity.

Let's look at Moses. Moses progressed in the "more excellent way". Every prophet should not be content to abide outside of the tabernacle where the world congregates in the Outer Court. The Outer Court should be viewed only as a "passing through" area. When we enter the Holy Place, we see the great veil that divides us from the Holy of Holies. The Holy Place is somewhat glorious. The Holy Place will bring us as prophets to a place of unity and testimony, yet we know that behind the veil is where we see God and experience God in the FACE TO FACE Anointing. The Face to Face Anointing is an experience that I will share at a later time.

When a Prophets life abides in the Holy of Holies, that life is a walk that is FULLY RIPENED FRUIT. Moses is an example of this. Moses, walking in total obedience to the will of God and His Word, saw himself being matured. His being matured pushed him into trust with God. The difference today is that many prophets did not see themselves this way. They want to achieve full communion with God but, try as we might, none of us have reached the level of Moses

.

Let's look at the question of why? Understand that Moses was, also in his own consciousness, not an entity separate from God. He was never overwhelmed, but He could easily relate to the words God spoke to him. Prophets take note that even in our prophetic duties, God is more concerned with the messenger than the message? If the prophet is wrong, the prophetic message will be wrong too. This is what Moses understood. God is more concerned that we embody the message than that we preserve our reputation as prophets.

What you will come to understand as you mature in the prophetic is that as helpful as the prophetic is to the church, the saints, church folks or the Christians are not willing to embrace all who claim to speak on behalf of God. The church and the Body of Christ must "test the spirits to see whether they are from God, because many false prophets have gone out into the world" (1 John 4:1). The Apostle John is concerned with whether the "prophet" affirms the incarnation of God the Son in the person of Jesus Christ (1 John 4:2–3; 2 John 7–11). He writes that "It is the Spirit of prophecy who bears testimony to Jesus" (Rev. 19:10). In other words, all true prophecy bears witness to Jesus Christ. This is not debatable.

Prophetic revelation is not only rooted in the gospel of the life, death, and resurrection of Jesus, but also to bear witness to the person of the incarnate Christ. Prophecy, therefore, is fundamentally Christ-centered.

Today, unlike Moses, we struggle greatly to become one with God's directives and our prophetic utterances are not always pointing to Christ. With Moses the actual prophetic word always overwhelmed him and upon its conclusion he would need to step back and examine the vision he had received. This is a great prophetic habit that we all should practice. Moses would constantly examine himself. Today as prophets we tend to transmit the prophetic in our own words. Like Moses our prophetic utterance must become prophecy that acts like our technology. The "live feed" option must be God's words being broadcast.

The fruit we bear in the prophetic ministry comes as a natural by-product of our roots abiding in the relationship with God (John 15). 1 Corinthians 14:1 says that we are to desire earnestly spiritual gifts but especially prophecy. The prophet Isaiah referred to the prophets as the eyes of Israel (Isaiah 29:10). Prophets can "see" things on a regular basis that others don't. Prophets have absolutely no power. All that is accomplished must be done by the Holy Spirit's power through the prophet. We must never forget this, prophets.

Once a prophet is convinced of the value of the prophetic ministry in their personal lives and in the Body of Christ, they then become relevant. Once Moses was convinced, he became the preeminent prophet of God. A prophet that knows that he or she is accepted by God is free from the fear of man. This is something that we all must come to understand. This was the temperament of Moses. Knowing in our inner man (spirit man) how much we are loved by the Father fills the need we all have for affirmation and glory (John 5:44). Knowing that our Heavenly Father loves us produces rest of the soul. This allows us as prophets to flow prophetically out of an overflow on a regular basis, and thus we avoid worn out prophetic utterances that we hear over and over again. God is a communicator with his prophets and has an abundance of things to say if we will learn his mode of operation. This blew my mind when I realized it. Prophets, to the extent that we neglect this fact, we will fail. Biblical prophets were individuals of wisdom, counsel, insight, and discipline. Prophets today need to understand that our training is as much in life as in the classroom.

When we speak of a school for prophets, it means a specialized type of training ground which prepares prophets for the Body of Christ as a whole and to foster, appreciate, understand, and nurture the budding prophets. The School of the Prophet is

the place of grace, where prophets of today come into an understanding that the inner man, or spirit man, develops when the
mind of the prophet is unoccupied by the cares of waking consciousness, when it is quietly at rest, untroubled by the thoughts
that fill it at other times, then the Spirit of God takes full and
complete possession, and causes to pass before it the ideas or
the images of thought that constitute the divine revelation to be
made. The atmosphere becomes a platform for the divine presence to birth the inner man and teach it about Godly control.
This control is always complete and compelling. Under it, the
prophet becomes the one moved, not the mover, in the forma-
tion of his message. This is what Peter means in his well-known
declaration: "For no prophecy ever came by the will of man; but
men spake from God, being moved by the Holy Spirit" (2 Peter
1:21).

The honor of speaking on behalf of God comes from knowing
Him intimately and conveying His heart as well as His words.
Forty years Moses spends in the wilderness; he is healing, growing and maturing. Moses became an accurate and relevant
mouth-piece of God because he allowed God to deal with his inner being first. As God heals your heart of the pain of the past,
it enables you to speak more clearly and not through a filter of
hurt and bitterness.

So how do you develop you "Unseen Prophetic Life?" Soaking
in his presence is critical. Soaking will draw you to intimacy
with God. Soaking or laying in God's presence will sharpen your
sensitivity to the Holy Spirit, your prophetic gift will be intensi-
fied as well as your passion for Jesus. Developing your unseen

prophetic life also includes cultivating a hidden life in the Word. Knowing the scriptures enables you to know the character of God, the way He speaks and the parameters God has laid out for your prophetic ministry. We judge prophecy through the standard of the Word and through the fruit of the Spirit. Knowing this, every prophet can discard any words they receive that doesn't line up with the word of God.

Prophets, we also need to understand that our worship quiets our spirits and ushers us into the presence of the Lord where hearing comes much easier. Being a worshiper goes hand in hand with the prophetic ministry. When three kings confronted Elisha and asked for a word from the Lord, Elisha sent for a minstrel to stir up the prophetic gift within him. The company of prophets came down from the high places playing harps, tambourines, flutes and lyres before them as they were prophesying (1 Samuel 10:5).

Our intercessory life is important also as prophets since so much of what we receive is not meant to be shared but meant to be released back to Heaven in intercessory prayer. When we see something negative, God is showing us this to pray positively and speak His heart back to Him on the issue.

When the prophet is in right standing, our work is to call into line those who are out of line! Yes, this is unpopular because you will oppose the popular in morality and spirituality. For a relevant prophet, your degree of effectiveness is determined by your measure of unpopularity. Compromise is not known to you, and as you develop, you will realize this.

Prophets, as you develop your inner self, you will be seen as unquestionably controversial and unpardonably hostile. People will see you as you march to another drum. You will breathe the rarefied air of inspiration as you become a "seer" who comes to lead the blind. Your life now moves in the heights of God and comes into the valley with a "thus saith the Lord in Word and Deeds." You now come to understand that "prophetic isolation" is of God and you are to constantly be available to "repent, be reconciled to God!"

So what am I saying? Simply that our consciousness and the certainty of a prophet's inner man being developed is all about the manifestation of the Spirit of God within them. "Inspiration" is a term we use lightly, but it designates the divine origin of the anointing. The interior process of the Spirit's action upon the mind of the prophet is manifest from the authority with which they put forth the Word of God.

Even as inspired authors of the biblical books of the Bible, we see prophets, when they sat down to write the divine, the human elements in their mental action were perfectly harmonious and inseparable (Luke 1:3). This is what we see in the life of Moses and others. The fact of such inspiration is unmistakably presented in the Bible. Welcome to the mentality of a relevant prophet who is mature. We walk in the Spirit to the degree we talk to Him (Gal 5:16).

There are four stages that all prophets should adhere to to totally grow the inner prophetic man. This is your gateway to the supernatural as you will always need to pray continually to experience the growth needed for each new season of life. Let's look at these stages and apply them to our life.

STAGE #1: CONSTANT AND CONSISTENCY; EXPECTANCY OF PRAYER

Praying regularly with expectancy for the Father to strengthen you with might in the inner man or spirit man. As prophets we are to use God's strength to sustain righteous choices in our pursuit of 100-fold obedience (in all areas including finances, time, speech, eyes, and the like) which is required of all prophets who desire to experience more.

STAGE #2: MOVING WITH A TOTALLY CLEAN HEART

Moving with a totally clean heart prepares us to, in our hearts (mind/emotions), to experience more. Being rooted and grounded in His love is sweet and powerful. Experiencing His manifest presence sustains us through life's trials, so we can count it all joy and understand when God does something another way, we re-anchor ourselves in him to experience "his" more.

STAGE #3: THE MANTLE OF MOSES

This mantle is the newfound ability to comprehend (experience) God as he roots us and grounds us in Him more. When we as Prophets are exhilarated in God's love, we feel no need to seek our greatness in being successful in man's eyes. We find success,

identity and satisfaction in the ocean of God's love. Thus we inherit the Mantle of Moses.

STAGE #4: UNDERSTANDING THE NECESSITY OF WORK TO EXPERIENCE HIS PURPOSE IN EACH OF OUR NEW SEASONS

It took Moses years in the Wilderness to prepare for his next
season, and many times the prophet of today believes we can
achieve the necessary preparation in mere moments of time. We
want to totally fulfill God's purpose in each season of our life
in this age and the age-to-come but unless we pay the price of
Moses, we will not experience this growth.

These stages are the realization of our inner man or spirit
man that we must practice daily. This is who we are and the
responsibility we bear to produce, grow and mature our spirit
man.

CHAPTER EIGHT

Navy Seals and Prophets

"You Are A Professional For God, Act Like It"

You could have a politician, an entertainer, or some other big name that was chosen to give the graduation speech at your college. But you can't beat the advice you'd get from the Navy SEAL training. While many of you may find this strange, it's not that strange, really. Many of The modern day Commentary Prophets should learn these lessons. They are invaluable and needed now! As Prophets, we all are from very different backgrounds, but we can learn these ten basic, most important lessons from the result of completing the notoriously difficult SEAL training program.

In Navy SEAL training mentality is important, and the brain is the strongest muscle in the body. Stories of how combat soldiers have been shot repeatedly but were not aware of it until the fight was over are true. They were so focused on their duty and their assignment. The power to do such things comes from the mind and can be tapped into by practicing mental preparation which is a prophetic principle of training for the now generation prophets.

Joseph and Moses are classic examples as to how important mental preparedness is for surviving and enduring any challenging or life altering situation that you could encounter as a prophet. Let's look at the Navy SEAL's "Practice of Emergency Conditioning (EC): Makes the Unknown Familiar." Another name for this is faith fortified with Trust in God.

Emergency conditioning (EC) means conditioning the mind in advance of emergencies, thus producing psychological strength in times of crisis. This is also referred to as "battle-proofing" or "battle inoculation" by military personnel. As a Prophet you need to understand that you're called by God and not everyone is going to like or love you. You understand that your calling is for the service of God unto mankind. You are the exponent that God can send to an area, a ministry, a people that may reject God, and that means they reject you in rejecting God because you are his representative - his mouthpiece. You bring his message.

Here are ten things that we learn from Navy Seals that will benefit us as Prophets.

1. START THE DAY BY MAKING YOUR BED.

Is it surprising that a Navy SEAL commander will tell you what to do as a little kid? Start every day making your bed which was the first task of the day at SEAL training. If you do so, it will mean that the first thing you do in the morning is to accomplish something which sets the tone for the day, encourages you to accomplish more, and reinforces that little things in life matter. As a prophet you must accomplish the small things first like establishing a relationship with God. This will allow you to be able to know you have a foundation for your ministry. Every prophet of biblical relevance had a relationship with God. The relationship develops and matures the mentality of a prophet.

"Sometimes Navy SEALs have bad days, if by chance you have a miserable day, you will come home to a bed that is made, that you made," "and a made bed gives you encouragement that tomorrow will be better." As a Prophet some days will be better than others, but the mentality you develop through the relationship with Christ will help you to stand. Moses, Elijah, Elisha, Samuel, and Joseph, just to name a few, all understood how important it is to accomplish something.

2. FIND THE RIGHT PEOPLE TO HELP YOU.

Each day, as part of Navy SEAL training, the volunteers have to paddle several miles down the coast in heavy surf, using small rubber boats. Everyone had to paddle together on a synchronized count and with similar strength. Otherwise the boats would "turn against the wave and be unceremoniously tossed back on the beach." That metaphor carries over into life, "For the boat to make it to its destination, everyone must paddle."

The point is that you can't change the world alone. You will need some help, and to truly get from your starting point to your destination takes help. The good will of God sent strangers to you who are being led by God. It's a small wonder why every prophet needs to find you a mentor that you can trust and will listen to.

There are some prophets with mentors who think they know more than their mentor or constantly do the opposite of your mentor's directions. They have the wrong mentor relationship. You're looking for a puppet and not a leader to help make you better. You will never find the Elijah or Moses that you need to develop. Don't get caught up here or you will move through a great portion of your life without growth.

3. ATTITUDE AND HEART CAN OUTWEIGH OTHER ADVANTAGES.

Looking at Seal training again, one of the toughest groups of SEALs was a boat crew of six men, none of whom was more than five feet five inches tall. The bigger students referred to them as "the munchkin crew." Simply enduring the training was proof of toughness. The munchkin crew was among just 35 men in the original class of 150 who stuck around, but the smaller guys "out paddled, out-ran, and out swam all the other boat crews."

What is the lesson here? "SEAL training was a great equalizer. Nothing mattered but your will to succeed. Not your color, not your ethnic background, not your education and not your social status. If you want to change the world, measure yourself or measure a person by the size of their heart, not the size of their flippers. As a prophet you either have the heart to move forward or you don't. This is not about your pastor, your family, your spouse, your church, your resources or your upbringing. This is about you wanting to or not wanting to develop as a prophet. The biblical schools of the prophets are the foundation platform of maturing gifts, not emotional outbursts based on personal preferences.

4.KEEP MOVING FORWARD.

Some of the most uncomfortable moments during SEAL training are when the students are punished for small infractions like having a smudge on a belt buckle during uniform inspections. A failing uniform inspection may mean the student has to run fully clothed into the surf zone and then, wet from head to toe, roll around on the beach until every part of your body was covered with sand. "Some call this the sugar cookie. What's funny is that you may have to stay in that uniform the rest of the day—cold, wet and sandy." Many students can't endure the pain. The key to succeeding was to accept that sometimes life just sucks, but you have to move forward. Prophets who say that they are called to prophetic ministry are going to experience the 'sugar cookie effect' in gossip, alienation, favoritism, and various forms of backlash in and out of the church. Can you stand to keep moving forward? Ezekiel, Isaiah, and Amos are classic examples of this and as a contemporary prophet, you will be also.

5.DON'T BE AFRAID OF THE CIRCUSES.

The "circuses" during SEAL training referred to remedial physical training—an extra two hours of calisthenics for failing to meet a standard during the day. Circuses were "designed to wear you down, to break your spirit, or to force you to quit." Nobody wanted to fail at anything; nobody wanted to have to go to the circus at the end of the day when they were already exhausted from training. As painful as it was, however, the extra two hours of working out started to pay off. The students who were "constantly on the list ... got stronger and stronger." Pain builds strength and resiliency, both in training and the real world. Don't be afraid of it.

Prophets, I can't stress this enough. If you're not willing to experience discomfort yourself, you're not worthy to carry the prophetic mantle. Again any relevant prophet of God went through some sort of hell from personal life to spiritual life. The challenges were beyond the scoop of endurance but they made it and God was glorified in their life, despite the issues. Joseph is the poster child but there is also Abraham, Moses, and this list goes on and on. Can we add your name to the list!

6.BE RESOURCEFUL AND INNOVATIVE.

It probably won't surprise you to learn that SEAL training included an obstacle course. One of the obstacles is called the "slide for life" and consisted of a 200-foot rope stretched between a 30-foot high tower and a 10-foot high tower.

The record for completing the obstacle course had stood for years until a student in one class shattered the record, in part, by racing down the slide for life head-first instead of the slower, safer method that everyone else used. Taking risks and being innovative often pays off.

When you learn how to believe in what God has given you, you'll be different, unique, and most of all available to be used by God. Small wonder some prophets seems to move faster or develop in different degrees is because of this simple fact: they are willing to do what others aren't. It will pay off. Isaiah was willing to do; Jeremiah was willing also after he was assured by God. Can you say relationship again!

7.DON'T BACK DOWN FROM THE SHARKS.

The idea of volunteering for something like SEAL training may never appeal to you, but many of those to whom this does are confident that they have the right life choice. You must be this confident in your gifting, prophet.

The "night swim," concept in SEAL Training is one in which students have to swim through shark-infested waters. They assure you that no student has ever been eaten by a shark—at

least not recently. But, you are also taught that if a shark begins to circle your position, stand your ground. Do not swim away. Do not act afraid. And if the shark, hungry for a midnight snack, darts towards you, punch him in the snout and he will turn and swim away." The lesson here is that if you can face a shark alone in the Pacific Ocean, you can probably face most of life's other sharks. Don't be afraid of them.

Prophets, what are you afraid of - not being invited back, not being popular, not be able to do what you know you been called? Your faith is key; your relationship with God is priceless. There are many sharks in the body of Christ. That does not mean you run and hide every time someone does not receive you. You will always be in a night swim and this is one test you must pass. No exceptions!

8. BE YOUR VERY BEST IN YOUR DARKEST MOMENTS.

Among the many missions Navy SEALs tackle is to conduct underwater attacks against enemy ships. This involves a pair of SEAL divers swimming two miles underwater, "using nothing but a depth gauge and a compass to get to their target."

Most of the way during the swim, some light can reach the depths at which the SEALs are swimming. Close to the target, however, the shadow of the ship itself blocks all the light, and the SEALs find themselves working in pitch dark,. "Every SEAL knows that, the darkest moment of the mission is the time when you must be calm, composed—when all your tactical skills, your physical power and all your inner strength must be brought to bear."

Prophet, one of the greatest tools of Satan to silence you is to direct and distract others against you, especially people who don't know you! Satan wants to literally destroy your character and ruin your witness. When you're a prophet of whom God is guiding and you're under attack, that is when you must be at your very best! If you are of any relevance you will have critics, haters, and those who are simply on assignment for your destruction. Their efforts will demand the best of God within you!

The children of Israel who saw Moses as an unfit weak leader after the twelve went up to see the land God had given them saw Moses at his best when he saved their lives from the wrath of God.

9. SING WHEN YOU'RE UP TO YOUR NECK IN MUD.

"Hell Week" is the ninth week of SEAL training. It involves six days of almost no sleep and constant physical challenges. Part of this takes place at a swampy area like the one between San Diego and Tijuana known as the Mud Flats. Here is where we see the instructors ordering the class into the freezing mud for hours, which "consumed each man until there was nothing visible but their heads. The instructors will then allow you to leave the mud. Sometimes people do quit."

There is a legendary story of a man in the group who started singing. Another joined in, and then another. The instructors threatened them, but they kept singing, which made the whole exercise just bearable enough to finish. This is what a mental edge is all about. Do you have this type of mentality?

Your mentality can't be stressed enough. Scripture says as we think so we are. Physical/mental challenges are quick to take prophets out of the arena. What are you willing to endure for the Glory of God. Joseph endured numerous challenges and yet there was a song in his heart that pushed him despite? Do you have a song, prophet? Let's sing it now!

10. NEVER QUIT. (NEVER "RING THE BELL.")

In SEAL training, students can quit anytime and many ultimately do. There is a brass bell at the center of the training compound, and if you decide you want out of the course, all you have to do is go up to it and ring it.

Ring the bell, and you no longer have to wake up at 5 o'clock. Ring the bell, and you no longer have to do the freezing cold swims. Ring the bell, and you no longer have to do the runs, the obstacle course, the PT, and you no longer have to endure the hardships of training. Just ring the bell. The ultimate key to success is never to ring the bell.

Those prophets who will ultimately succeed in their ministries will not quit. They will endure, adjust and move forward as they know that this is their life and they will do what is necessary, not what many sees as fashionable. This type of prophet does not have to be coached over and over to pay the price. They will pay it as they realize it is the seed of anointed manifestation.

This is the reason why our group of God gifted individuals called prophets are to be respected as one way or another. The cost of this anointing is great and it's paid in uncomfortable settings, over long periods of time, under what appears to be mundane conditions. You can't quit. You will regret it. Trust God enough to see it through

.

CHAPTER NINE

Forgetting That Which Is behind. The Initial Test Of The Prophet

"Test Every Prophet Must Pass"

How we respond to the situations of life, whether pleasant or painful, reflects on who we are. As a prophet your response will expose your true spiritual condition. It is critical that our response reveals our beliefs, values, priorities, and our spiritual conditions and focus at any particular moment because of who we are: prophets of God.

Peter called the trials of life as "the proof of your faith" in 1 Peter 1:7. "Proof" is Greek for dokimion, a word used of the smelting process for refining and testing precious metals to either remove the impurities or prove the quality of the metal. Dokimion comes from a word group that was used of the test or trial itself, or of the results, the proof, the pure gold that was left.[5]

As we focus on the life of Elisha, we see Elisha readily does his daily work with great elegance. When the moment of God's call comes, he is ready to jump on it. The history of Elisha's family lets us know that our upbringing does play a role in life's tests. We see that Elisha's father was a wealthy farmer, a man whose household was among the number that in a time of almost universal apostasy had not bowed the knee to Baal. Theirs was a home where God was honored and where allegiance to the faith of ancient Israel was the rule of daily life.

The early years of Elisha were in the quietude of country life and the discipline of useful work. He received the training in habits of simplicity and of obedience to his parents and to God that helped to fit him for the high position he was to occupy. Yes, this was a vital part of the early training of Elisha. He was passing his initial tests. While it looked like a boring life, this is the initial test of a prophet. The actual test was simply learning. My how difficult we ourselves make our lives sometimes!

The actual prophetic call came to Elisha while, with his father's servants, he was plowing in the field. He had taken up the work that lay nearest. He possessed both the capabilities of a leader among men and the meekness of one who is ready to serve. Of a quiet and gentle spirit, he was nevertheless energetic and steadfast. Integrity, honor, and the love and fear of God were his, and in the humble round of daily toil he gained strength of purpose and nobleness of character, constantly increasing in grace and knowledge. While co-operating with his father in the home-life duties, he was learning to co-operate with God. These were his initial tests. We have to now distinguish what our initial tests are.

By faithfulness in little things, Elisha was preparing for weightier assignments. Day by day, through practical experience, he gained a fitness for a broader, higher work. He learned to serve; in learning this, he learned also how to instruct and lead. The lesson is for all.

None can know what may be God's purpose in His discipline, but every prophet can and may be certain that faithfulness in little things is the evidence of fitness for greater responsibilities. Every act of our lives is a revelation of character, and we as prophets, only in small duties, prove ourselves worthy to be God's prophets. "A workman that needn't not to be ashamed" can be honored by God with higher service (2 Timothy 2:15). We as prophets are the work men and work women of God.

A prophet who feels that it is of no consequence how he performs the smaller tasks proves himself unfit for a more honored position. He may think himself fully competent to take up the larger duties, but God looks deeper than the surface. I'm convinced that the quicker we learn and appreciate this fact, the quicker we will grow and develop individually.

Elisha's readiness to serve God's call represents a path of symbolic boots which represent "readiness for the gospel of peace (Eph. 6:15)." Elisha knows he is destined for duty because of his relationship with God. He is following through on his daily commitments to his family, but when the prophet comes knocking, he is ready to spring up and take action.

He responds to God's call with a willing and generous heart. To solidify his new commitment to God's call, Elisha destroys his former means of substance, the oxen themselves. He isn't just throwing a big dinner for the neighbors, but putting his money where his mouth is. When he slaughters the oxen, it becomes clear that he is embarking on a new way of life and cannot easily return to the old.

This is not the act of a coward; this is the act of a driven determined individual who understands the moment he has arrived to in his life. This act symbolizes his commitment to prophetic ministry as we see him willing to take what he has and lay it to the side for the work of God. Today, how many of us are really willing to lay aside anything for the work of God? This is what is required of the prophet. He is passing an initial test that makes him fit to serve. We must stop talking about what an honor it is to serve and we have no commitment to do as such. This is a disgrace to the calling and can't be honored any more.

My question to you is this: How far do you want to go in God? Please understand that this will depend on how you respond to the tests. Luke 9:62 says, "No one who puts his hand to the plow and looks back is fit for service in the kingdom of God." The example of Elisha and Elijah is a great standard bearer for prophets. Like Elisha your initial test in your calling will be what are you willing to leave behind. Will you leave everything behind that God calls for or will you pick and choose as you see fit, or trust God, or his sent representative.

1 Kings 19:19-21 is where Elijah got his commission to raise up Elisha. God told him to go and receive Elisha son of Shaphat as a Prophet. Here we have the start of 60 years of ministry. What a legacy we see as Elisha is plowing with twelve yoke of oxen, and he himself was driving the twelfth pair. Elijah went up to him and threw his mantle upon him.

Elisha then left his oxen and ran after Elijah. "Let me kiss my father and mother good-by," he said, "and then I will come with you. Go back." This is a critical initial test of Elisha. When God calls a prophet he or she will be initially tested. Elisha wants to go with Elijah, but Elijah says, "Go back." My brother or sister prophet, are you ready for this type of testing?

Elijah replied. "What have I done to you?" So Elisha left him and went back. He took his yoke of oxen and slaughtered them.

He burned the plowing equipment to cook the meat and gave it to the people he was working with.

Elisha is dedicated to passing his test, because he knows this is his time, his moment. As we think about ourselves, how many of us know this is our time, this is our initial test, we must pass?

One thing I must mention is that Elisha knew who Elijah was because of his "mantle". It provides the key. Elijah's mantle (clothing in the natural and gift in the spiritual sense) indicated he was a prophet. So when Elijah comes up and throws his mantle around Elisha, Elisha didn't have to ask 'what's going on?' He knew exactly what that meant. Mantles were typically made of animal hair and were generally worn by kings and prophets. They were symbolic of the owners calling, position, and authority. So Elisha knew. This was a passing of the test of Elijah's calling and position onto Elisha as the next prophet.

Elisha interprets Elijah's action as a request to become his servant (prophet in training). Notice that he asks permission to go say good bye to his parents and then he will follow. Elijah clearly lets him know that, "No one is stopping you Elisha! What have I done that you would make such a request?" Elisha goes back, kills the oxen, and uses the yoke to boil the animals for a meal with the "people" Then he follows Elijah as his servant. Can you imagine what is on his mind as he ponders his life? His relationship with God dictates a calmness as he handles his tests.

Elisha's service with Elijah and paves the way for his future prophetic role. There is no doubt about it. What transpires sounds similar to the occasion Jesus declared, "follow me", to some would be disciples.

There was one who asked to go bury his father first. Jesus said, "Let the dead bury the dead" in Matt 8:21. Do you see the attention to servanthood and the importance of the initial test of it? This is really serious business. Having the right mentality is everything. Jesus is saying let the spiritually dead bury the physically dead, but the reality is that they were really offering an excuse to Jesus' call to discipleship. How many times do we see this today in the body of Christ?

Luke 9:61 says the potential disciple promises to follow Jesus but wants to say farewell to his family. Jesus answers in words that remind us of Elisha plowing: "No one who puts a hand to the plow and looks back is fit for the kingdom of God "(Luke 9:62)." Elisha followed and as tough as this sounds we should know that the enemy we will face will not care or wait for us to be ready to deal with him. That is our responsibility to be ready and prepared. This is a call to action, not us declaring we are prophets and then doing nothing.

As prophets, we must spend time counting the cost. This will help us to understand. We see the seriousness of Elisha's response. When Elisha received his call as the mantle of Elijah touched his shoulders, he knew it contained a promise of the endowment of the power of God. This became his cherished hope, in his heart. This was not a game, nor a self-anointing it was his commissioning.

Let's also look ourselves to see how serious we are and how we have handled our business. How seriously did Elisha take this call from Elijah? We see that Elisha slaughtered his oxen as a sacrifice and burnt the plowing equipment to cook the meat! He knew he has been called and there was no going back; NONE. We see a great example of someone leaving behind the old life when the call of God comes. When you take on the mantle of a prophet, be a prophet, Don't change per your company or audience to be accepted. This is the reality of our today generation.

Elisha knew this was a new beginning for him and there was no compromise with his past life. This is the prophetic mentality we must have if we are going to walk in the prophetic office of a prophet. Let me say again that Luke 9:62 says "No one who puts his hand to the plow and looks back is fit for service in the kingdom of God." How about you Prophet? Have you been looking back or are you pressing on to the higher calling of our Lord?

There is no doubt that as we read about these two, the ministries of Elijah and Elisha supplement each other, but they are different. God uses different personalities. God uses different kinds of prophets (servants) in different ways and at particular times.

Here we see two different kinds of prophets. There is also a spiritual signification of the number two. Whereas one denotes there is no other, two affirms there is another and therefore a difference. The two, though different in character, may be one in testimony and friendship.

Prophets today need to understand that we all are different, but we are called by God to work together. Throughout the scriptures we will find two persons linked together to present a contrast: as in such cases as Abraham and Lot, Ishmael and Isaac, Jacob and Esau. There are also two bearing witness to the truth as Enoch and Noah, Moses and Aaron, Caleb and Joshua, Naomi and Ruth, Ezra and Nehemiah. You'll also find, the sending forth of the Apostles by twos, Mark 6:7 and Rev. 11:3. The very difference you see in another prophet is a test you must pass in learning how to work with and being empowered by that prophet.

When we consider that with such a call as what Elisha received to succeed the great prophet Elijah, one would imagine that he would soon become quite prominent. This is one of the great problems of today's prophets as we run from ministry to ministry looking for notoriety and not learning stability. We would rather skip the testing time. There is no wonder we never learn how to pass our initial tests.

We fail to see that God, however, does not work that way. The first job the young prophet Elisha got was to be the serving man to his master. In 2 Kings 3:11-12 we read that Elisha "poured water on the hands of Elijah." He waited on him, brought the wash basin, drew the water, and thus had a future career of great usefulness began. This is the test after the test after the test. Your mantle, your gift, your servitude must be sure, tried and tested.

As we look at the later results, Elisha must have been faithful and observant, gradually becoming qualified. He got the double portion, didn't he?

Let us learn the lesson. The call of God is often times thrilling. We run over with enthusiasm and feel that the time is short and we must be up and doing. Everybody responds so differently, because we are just that: different. As prophets we will need to be stirred.

We as God's prophets must learn that we have to mark time and accept the chastening of our eager spirits, until we are really ready. Prophet you are then on your way to your next test. This is the test that most prophets never accept or fulfill because it is boring, time consuming and we find ourselves with an unnamed ministry for long stretches in our life. Welcome to the building of your mantle, the foundation, of God's work upon your life.

Understand that tests will be a part of your life as a prophet. The day arrived that Elijah should be removed. Elisha made a decision from which he would not be shaken. He was going to stay by his master at all costs. Here we have yet another test: the test of transition.

Elijah tried to shake Elisha off, but the only response Elijah got was, "As the LORD liveth, and as thy soul liveth, I, (Elisha) will not leave thee." Three times he was advised to stay behind, but each time he made the same reply.

As prophets we set our faces to seek God and then we get turned aside by some distraction. Then we soon discover that we have let God down and are getting nowhere. We are failing the test. This is for many of our greatest challenge.

Elisha's determination is given as a lesson in, that we too should diligently seek. Christ taught the same thing. In Luke chapters 11 and 18, we are urged to ask, seek, and knock. Chapter 18 shows diligence as the widow who wanted action by the unjust judge. Change comes through diligence. Who among us is praying without quitting or pursuing despite the results you are currently seeing?

Elisha wanted the anointing of the Spirit. Elisha's last journey with Elijah contains some good lessons of illustration of what transpires in the heart when one is tarrying for the baptism with the Spirit.

Let's look at four areas. Starting at Gilgal, which means rolling away, we get rid of the worldly way of leaning on the arm of flesh, and begin a new separated walk in which Christ will prove Himself as "all and in all." This is faith in action.

Then we come to Bethel, the house of God. This teaches abiding. The Spirit-filled life can be lived in no other way, and the sooner we learn it the better. This is the area of decision, and Elijah would never shake him, until God took him.

Jericho was their next stop. Here we are introduced to the "obedience of faith." If God is to work, we must believe. There is no other way. We pray and pray and do all we can to get the baptism, but faith and praise will make more headway than anything else. This is the warfare area as Elisha is being processed.

Jordan is the last call. The plan of God is death to self, or, "Not by might, nor by power, but by the Spirit, saith the Lord of hosts." Jordan is crossed; Elisha is still following Elijah. This is when we learn to see!

Remember these four areas. They are areas that will be the foundation of your tests over and over as you will cycle in and out of these four areas as you move from test to test from one level of Glory to another in God.

The moment arrives with the offer: "Ask what I shall do for thee, before I be taken from thee." The young man seizes his opportunity and claims what goes with his call: "I pray thee, let a double portion of thy spirit be upon me." What he wanted was the portion of the eldest son who now is to become the head of the sons of the prophets. He is within his rights and he knows who he has become to Elijah. The custom of the times was to give the eldest son a double portion of the inheritance, for he became the head of the house when the father died. Elijah, as father, was to be taken, and Elisha must now have what goes with his new position.

Elisha had trained in the shadow of the great Elijah. Yet he impacted a larger population with his ministry than his master did as the stories of Elisha's ministry extend from 2 Kings 2-9 and 13.

WHAT CAN WE AS PROPHETS LEARN FROM THE CALL AND TESTING OF ELISHA?

1.It always costs something to follow the call to God. To walk this path is seldom easy, but most of the time it is fulfilling. Stop running from tests

2. Elisha needed to learn for himself that God was the real power in ministry. It is so easy to connect symbols with power, like a mantle, ordination, ministry position, or a successful program, when it is really the work of God through you or your position or your program for the work of God.

3. What is "seen" is easier to identify than the invisible Spirit of God. Elisha's struck the Jordan and nothing happened. His mentor knew where the real power came from God. The second time he struck the river the waters parted. Elisha gained the most important knowledge anyone in ministry will ever grasp, and many never will.

Empowerment does not come from degrees, positions, mentors, or ordination credentials, but from the Lord through his special servants.

CHAPTER TEN

Removing Hindrances To Prophetic Decrees

"What's In The Way?"

When a prophet moves into the prophetic office, they will be led to speak forth decrees instead of just words of knowledge and general prophecy. God will use you to... "Use your prophetic authority to decree the will of God into the earth."

Prophets understand that there is power and authority in the decree of the prophet and you will have to ability to release or activate a person into prophetic office through prophetic decree or if you have an apostolic mantle, you will be able to open that door for the Body of Christ through apostolic decree.

Prophets make prophetic decrees and proclamations into the heavens daily. Words release life or death to us and our families. What we do not know can kill us. The saying that "Sticks and stones may break my bones, but words will never hurt me" is not true. The most powerful words that affect our life are the words we speak. Proverbs 18:21 says that "Death and life are in the power of the tongue."

Paul understood that the Word is to be spoken out of his mouth to set the cornerstones of his life, and since we have the same spirit of faith, according to what is written, "I believed and therefore I spoke," we also believe and therefore speak (2 Corinthians 4:13).

SPIRITUAL WARFARE: INTERCESSION AND PROPHETIC DECREES.

Doors are open and shut in the spirit realm to angels and demons as well as in the natural realm to people. In both realms, the doors are open or shut by believers speaking God's Word. "I will give you the keys of the kingdom of heaven, and whatever you bind on earth will be bound in heaven, and whatever you loose on earth will be loosed in heaven" (Matthew 16:19).

The power of the spirit realm impacts the earth according to the actions and words of people especially you the prophet. Ask

Him to release angels to go and get what God has for us. Part of the angelic job description is that of bringing us what is rightfully ours. The angels must be sent out to battle the forces of the enemy who is trying to keep us from our destiny.

Jeremiah Chapter 1 tells us that the purpose of the word of the Lord is to build, plant, root-up, and pull down. So when God gives you a revelation of something that comes out of heaven, it's for you to build. When God gives you a revelation, a promise that comes out of heaven, you are called to build, plant, loose, birth and bring to pass that word by working with the Holy Ghost. At the same time, you might have to pull some things down (in the spirit) that are opposing the fulfillment of your word.

Matt 16: "I say to you Peter, on this rock I will build My church, and the gates of Hades shall not prevail against it." Now what does Jesus mean by the words "on this rock?" Upon this rock-the rock of revelation I am building. Upon the rock of being able to hear what your Father in heaven is saying. In that same passage, Jesus goes on to say, "Peter, I've given you the keys-the keys to the kingdom." You know what the keys are? They are every prophetic words that you have. The keys are every revelation you've received. Some of us in the body of Christ are running around with a key chain full of keys, like a janitor, with keys jingling wherever we go. We don't trust the keys to work for us.

5 STEPS TO STOP HINDRANCES TO PROPHETIC DECREES:

1. Listen, heed, be obedient, and walk out what God has for you. Too many people, including the prophets, wonder why their dreams have not been fulfilled. The problem is that we have a lot of people in the body of Christ with good intentions who never walk out what God has for them. You need to understand that when God says something about you, He is speaking out and releasing your potential. God wants you to get excited and press on toward the mark of what He said you will be. Many people will get to heaven and find out how much more God had for them when they were on the earth, because they did not listen to the prophetic word. Listen and heed the word. Learn how to act like it is already so. Many people, to include the prophets, don't realize that most prophetic words, or their timing, are conditional upon us taking certain steps of obedience.

2. PROPHETS DEPLOY SPIRITUAL WARFARE. IDENTIFY YOUR PRINCE OF PERSIA.

There is a Prince of Persia in the spiritual realm holding up your blessings. Some of you have prayed for blessings, some even know that they should be blessed or further along but don't know why? It's not God. It's not you. It's the devil resisting your destiny, tying it up in the spirit. It happened to Daniel, it can happen to you. God had to send the Archangel Michael to battle through that prince of the enemy.

The same devil who came against Jesus and against Moses, he is warring against you. The devil wants to kill every move of God in its infancy. He wants to discourage you right when you get saved or right when you get healed. He wants to try taking God's blessings from you.

The devil knew the prophetic words about Jesus, so he said, "We need to issue a decree. We need to kill all the male children under two years old." It had been spoken that a deliverer was coming to Egypt. Satan knew the deliverer was coming. We are going to kill him." That's when God had to orchestrate the deliverance of the baby Moses. After that attempt on Moses' life, according to the book of Revelation, the devil was going to try killing all the offspring of women. That's you and that's me! Satan knows that God has a plan for us.

Satan has a plan of destruction. He is not just going to lie down, roll over and let you be what God wants you to be. He is working overtime to distract you and to delay the fulfillment of your promises. He is working overtime to side-line you or to kill, steal and destroy in your life. Demonic cohorts have been assigned to keep you from finding the revelation of God's will. And when you find it, he stirs up a lot of mess to get you so distracted that you can't really press on "toward the goal for the prize of the upward call of God in Christ Jesus." He is trying to get you into debt and into immoral relationships; he'll try any way he can to mess up your life.

You need to realize that there are Princes of Persia in the spiritual realm working to prevent you coming into the revelation and reality of your destiny. Something that God wanted to give you 21 days ago may be tied up—we need to release spiritual warfare and pray: "My God, I ask for the angelic host to resist the enemy's assignments that are keeping back what you promised me in the area of my finances."

Scripture tells us that we don't wrestle against flesh and blood, but demonic powers and principalities. We need to have our eyes opened to what is going on in the heavens. There is not a devil under every bush, but there are more devils under bushes than many Christians have been willing to admit. I'm not looking for demons. I don't have to look for them. They are there and I'm aware of them. I know that they want to destroy me but I'm neither afraid nor focused on that fact. I know who I am in Christ. We need to know our authority but we also need to be vigilant.

3. MAKE DECREES WITH AUTHORITY

Scripture calls New Testament believers priests and kings of the Most High God! What do you think begins to happen when you actually say something into the spiritual realm and make known the manifold wisdom of God to demonic powers and principalities? The enemy knows if you're unsure of your authority. You really need to have a revelation of who you are in Christ and that He, the hope of glory, lives in you. When you know your authority and make decrees, the enemy cannot invade your house. The angelic hosts of heaven and Jesus Himself will back up your decrees which line up with His prophetic or scriptural words to you.

You have been given kingly anointing and authority; you've been made to sit in heavenly places (Eph. 2:6). Every devil in hell trembles at your words when you know your position in Christ!

He knows that behind everything you say is the authority of heaven and Jesus Christ. The angels of God will come and arrest them. God begins to release angels to carry out His word in our life when we begin to release the word into heaven. We can actually aid in spiritual warfare.

"And Elijah the Tishbite, of the inhabitants of Gilead, said to Ahab, 'As the LORD God of Israel lives, before whom I stand, there shall not be dew nor rain these years, except at my word (1 Kings 17:1)." Notice that it was at the word of Elijah that there would be no dew or rain. Yes, it was the word of Elijah, but where did the word originate? The story continues: "It came to pass after many days, the word of the Lord came to Elijah, in the third year, saying, 'Go present yourself to Ahab. I will send rain on the earth'" So Elijah went to Ahab and said something like: "There won't be any dew or rain on the earth for years, except at my word, because God said that He is about to send a drought."

Elijah is only saying what God said—that is where his authority came from! Elijah partnered with God to see God's word fulfilled. Later, when God was about to send rain to the earth, He told the prophet to decree what He was about to do. Elijah had a place in fulfilling the word; he needed to release it before anything would happen.

As a result of Elijah's words, he heard the sound of abundant rain in the spirit. Now think about your situation—maybe God has said something about you but you didn't say anything to open up heaven so His word could come to pass. Have you heard the sound of the abundance of rain yet? Is there a sound in your spirit? God is waiting for you. Something about your word when you speak faith releases God's word and opens up the heavens. Then God can release the angels to do what He said He would do.

4. ALERT PEOPLE OF THEIR RESPONSIBILITY TO PROPHETIC DECREES."BIRTHING"

The responsibility of warfare and for fulfillment is not the prophets. You are the mouth piece, prophet your job is the teach people how to be a partner with God. The book of James says, "The effective, fervent prayer of a righteous man avails much (James 5:16b)."Our righteousness comes through faith in Christ and we need to speak from that authority. Prophets, when people tell you that "You know how many times I've prayed the word of the Lord and haven't seen anything!"

Remind them of this that Elijah discovered. Elijah realized that he needed to birth the word of God: "So Ahab went up to eat and drink. And Elijah went up to the top of Carmel; (and) bowed down on the ground... (a birthing position)" (I Kings 18:42)." Then he heard the sound. Elijah realized "This thing is not going to come to pass except at my word. Elijah realized that he had God's word. Then he said to his servant, "Go look. Do you see anything?" His servant looked and said, "I don't see anything." Elijah said to the servant, "Go look again." He is birthing. He said, "Ok, go again." He came back saying, "I don't see anything." But Elijah kept telling him to go back and look again. Eventually, after the seventh time, the servant saw the answer begin to manifest!

Elijah realized that he needed to pray the word through and take care of any opposition to its fulfillment. He began to release that word towards heaven, call it out of the spirit and call those things that were not as though they were, until they came into existence. He persisted even when he didn't see anything. Eventually, after the seventh time, he saw a cloud the size of a man's hand.

It's now time for you to release some words of destiny into the heavenly realm. It's time to decree what God has promised you and what He has said about you. It's time to declare what the Bible and the prophetic words have said about you. You are going to make powerful prayers of proclamation, of decree. This is how the prophet births the word into a person's life: by alerting them of their responsibility of the prophetic decree and, never allowing them to give up. This was a lesson for Elijah's servant as much as it was for him as he learned that perseverance is critical.

5. REMIND THE DEVIL OF YOUR DESTINY

You are going to begin to remind the devils in the spirit realm about your destiny words from God. You might even know the ruling spirit that is keeping you from what God says is yours. Maybe God said He was going to release prosperity on you. Then you need to take your spiritual arrow, put it in your bow and say,

"Spirit of poverty, God has said I would prosper. His word is true and you will not hinder me." Then your arrow is released and WHAM! You can release some revival arrows and some miracle arrows. You can also release some arrows against religious spirits. Every arrow is a promise. You need to be involved. Let the Holy Spirit bring to the forefront of your mind every word that God has given you, right now. Let God remind you of every prophetic promise—those are your words and they have authority. They will come to pass as you decree them.

Say what God has said and make sure that hindering devil knows that you are taking authority! Shake the kingdom of darkness!   Proclaim liberty to the captives.   We are making the manifold wisdom of God by the church known unto demonic powers and principalities in the heavens. Prophet this is what your decree does.   The reason people speak against prophetic decrees is because they want to do what the prophets are doing but don't want to pay the price." Everybody wants what you've got, but they don't want to do what's needed to get it! Many Christians want to do great things for God, but they do nothing. They are just talkers. They've just got a lot of vision, but no sight of the process. Prophets, wake up; the Body of Christ needs you.

CHAPTER ELEVEN

Impact of Prophetic Discernment On A Prophet's Life

"A Priceless Gift So Few Develop"

Prophetic discernment is more than just a process. Prophetic discernment is the supernatural insight into the realm of "spirits". Prophetic discernment means to see or perceive; once this happens prophets must learn to speak not of what's discerned but what God says.[6] Prophetic discernment of spirits is the one spiritual gift that can and will present many challenges to prophets as they develop. This is a critical area of growth.

Isaiah 6:1 says "I saw the Lord sitting on a throne, high and lifted up, and the train of His robe filled the temple." The prophet saw by the gift of discerning of spirits, the ability to see into the spirit realm. Also John, on the Isle of Patmos, saw the Holy Spirit as seven spirits before the throne.

HOW DOES THIS PROPHETIC DISCERNMENT AFFECT THE WAY A PROPHET LIVES?

IN FOUR WAYS:

1. Prophetic discernment acts as a means of protection, guarding us from being deceived spiritually. It protects us from being blown away by the winds of false doctrine that makes central an element of the gospel that is peripheral or treating a particular application of Scripture as though it were Scripture's central message.

2. Prophetic Discernment also acts as an instrument of healing, when exercised in grace, the ability to diagnose the spiritual needs of others. This type of prophetic gift is able to penetrate into the heart issues someone else faces better than the person can do. This is in some ways a very dangerous gift with which God has entrusted them. But when exercised in love, prophetic discernment can be the surgical scalpel in spiritual surgery that makes healing possible.

3. Prophetic discernment functions as a key to deliverance freedom. Growth in prophetic discernment sets us free from bondage,

enabling us to distinguish practices that may be helpful in some circumstances from those that are mandated in all circumstances. Prophetic discernment enables the prophet to recognize that deliverance is essential to all who want it. Prophetic discernment will let you know that you are on the right track.

4. Prophetic discernment serves as a catalyst to spiritual development: "The mocker seeks wisdom and finds none, but knowledge comes easily to the discerning." (Proverbs 14:6) Why? Because the prophet who discerns goes to the heart of the matter. The prophet then knows all things have their common foundation in God. This, therefore, does not lead to increased frustration, but to a deeper recognition of the harmony of all God's works and words.

The question should now be how is prophetic discernment to be obtained? Just as Christ Himself did by the anointing of the Spirit, through our understanding of God's Word, by our experience of God's grace, and by the progressive unfolding to us of the true condition of our own hearts. This is a process of time and will vary from prophet to prophet in different manifestations. That is why prophets must and should pray, "I am your servant; give me discernment." (Ps. 119:125) Prophetic discernment is the gift that will distinguish prophets and seers in their ranks and capabilities. As we learn how to operate in the gift of prophet discernment, we must remember the following points, which are extremely important points to consider as we look to develop our prophetic mantles.

1. As a prophet, you must learn how to Exercise and Test The gift: Hebrews 5:14 "But Good Food is for the mature, who because of practice have their senses trained to discern good and evil." Do not assure everything you see is of God. Test the spirit according to 1 John 4:1-3 to determine what is God and what is not. Prophet, reread this, again 7 times before you read # 2.

2. Examine the Visions or Situations thoroughly. Does is draw people to God or drive them away? Matthew 7:16-20 says know them by the fruit they bear. Not by if you are suspicious of what they bear. Our gifts are for the Glory of God, and wisdom is the key to know how God is deploying us for his Glory! Prophet, reread this again 7 times before you continue.

First Corinthians 10-11 says "to another the working of miracles, to another prophecy, to another distinguishing between spirits, to another speaking in various tongues, and to still another the interpretation of tongues. All these are the work of one and the same Spirit, who apportions them to each one as He determines."

Today we see demonic manifestations in Body of Christ seeming to thrive as the gift of discerning of spirits has not functioned among The five-Fold Ministry leaders to include the prophets.

The prophetic gift of discerning of spirits reveals the "kind" of spirit behind a supernatural manifestation. Acts 16:16-19 reads, "Now it happened as we went to prayer, that a certain slave girl possessed with a spirit of divination met us, who brought her masters much profit by fortune-telling. This girl followed Paul and us, and cried out, saying, 'These men are the servants of the Most High God, who proclaim to us the way of salvation.' And this she did for many days. But Paul, greatly annoyed, turned and said to the spirit, 'I command you in the name of Jesus Christ to come out of her.' And he came out that very hour."

The Lord revealed to Paul and his companions by the discerning of spirits that the slave girl in their midst was possessed with a spirit of divination. Paul did not speak to the woman, but he spoke directly to the spirit that had possessed her. He commanded the spirit of divination to come out of her, and that evil spirit obeyed his command. Why? Paul was anointed with the power of the Holy Spirit. He wasn't just a hearer of the word; he was a doer of the word.

Prophetic discernment identifies the gift in operation employing the "discernment of spirits" or "distinguishing between spirits." The Greek word for the gift of discernment is diakrisis.[7] The word describes being able to distinguish, discern, judge or appraise a person, statement, situation, or environment. In the New Testament it describes the ability to distinguish between spirits as in 1 Corinthians 12:10, and to discern good and evil as in Hebrews 5:14.

The Holy Spirit gives the gift of discernment to enable some prophets to clearly recognize and distinguish between the influence of God, Satan, the world, and the flesh in a given situation.

This will vary from prophet to prophet and prophetic experience is a foundation of developing this gift.

'Discernment' is sometimes used as a catch-word for speaking against others, or to defeat them in a struggle for power or influence, or just to pick at them until they quit or retreat. Discerning eyes look for whether something that's labeled 'discernment' is done from love, or whether it just is a clanging gong or a noisy cymbal. Jesus didn't call us to love ideas. He called us to love people. John put it as bluntly as he could: "One who does not love does not know God, for God is love (I John 4:8)."

When discerning, prophets need to keep in mind why he/she is doing it. Ask yourself, "If I raise this issue, how am I pointing people to Christ? How am I helping them grow in the Spirit? In what way am I loving them?"

If there's no answer to those questions, or if you have to stretch far and wide to come up with a complicated or weak answer, then it's best not to speak. Indeed, it›s time to focus on prayer and listening, because it may be your time to learn. Keep in mind you have not seen every type of prophet or prophetic manifestation. You need this type of experience so you can grow.

Prophetic discernment of spirits is the one spiritual gift that can and will present many challenges to prophets as they develop. Consider prophets the signs in your life of prophetic discernment.

1. DESIRE FOR THE GIFT (1 COR 14:1).

As with other spiritual gifts, desire is often the first sign of a gift of discernment of spirits... You may have a longing to see people set free from demonic bondage.... You may want to be more effective in prayer and spiritual warfare.... You may have a desire for holiness.... You may simply be curious about the spiritual realm.

2. LOVE FOR GOD'S PRESENCE

Prophets will have a passion for the un-grieved presence of the Holy Spirit in their lives. The highest use of the gift of discernment is not to see what the enemy is doing, but to discern what the Spirit of God is doing.

3. SENSITIVITY TO THE SPIRITUAL ATMOSPHERE

You're more sensitive to spiritual atmospheres than most other people. You may be affected adversely by the presence of any demonic activity in the environment around you. We live in a natural world and a spiritual world concurrently. When Jacob came across a group of angels, he named that place Mahanaim, meaning 'double camp (Gen 32:1-2). Like Jacob realized, we also live in a double camp where there is constant spiritual activity, and discerners have spiritual senses that are attuned to this.

4. FEELING DIFFERENT FROM OTHER PEOPLE

Most people in the body of Christ experience life through their natural senses. However, someone with an emerging prophetic gift of discernment of spirits can see and sense things that others do not see. This ability can result in you feeling different, lonely or misunderstood at times, especially when starting out. It is vital that someone with a developing prophetic gift of discernment finds a safe place to journey with others who are similarly gifted and accountable prophets.

5. UNUSUAL SIGNS

It is not uncommon for a prophet who is gifted in discernment to experience unusual events or manifestations. Prophets who are incubating a discernment gift begin to see or feel things that others are not aware of. This will result in unusual visions, dreams and sensations that alert them to what is happening in the spiritual realm.

6. CHILDHOOD / PRE SALVATION SIGNS.

It is not uncommon to experience things relating to your gift even before becoming a prophet. God prepares us for our calling and gifts from conception. Even when a talent or gift is misused, God can redeem it and anoint it for His use to serve Him and love and minister to others.

7. ABILITY TO KNOW WHAT LIES BEHIND A PERSON'S WORDS OR ACTIONS

Prophets with a gift of discernment has the ability to see behind what a person is saying and presenting. You may know whether

they are telling the truth or not. You may also recognize if someone is manifesting a demonic spirit and be able to identify what
that spirit is.

8. CONFIRMATION BY OTHERS AND LEADERS

You may have the gift confirmed through a prophecy given to
you. Sometimes prophetic gifts are identified through prophecy.
When you submit what you are seeing or sensing, your leaders
confirm your accuracy and your gift begins to be recognized for
its effectiveness. All Prophets need to understand that whenever
a gift is used to criticize or tear down a church, person or leader,
you know it is being misused, or is simply a prophet's hurt, frustration or agenda masquerading as discernment.

When you are judging and discerning prophecy, look for Love.
God is Love. He is your life and this earth life is not all there is,.
There is an eternal life of great dimension for every living soul.

Prophets, remember these things as we look for keys in developing prophetic discernment:

- It is governed by love, for if it is not, it's worthless (1
  Corinthians 13:1-3);
- It centers us onto Jesus the Christ and Lord (1 Cor 12:3),
  and His good news;
- It directs us to Scripture, not away from it (Isaiah 8:19, 20);
- It builds up the church and its members (Ephesians 4:11-
  12), giving it power, wisdom, character, boldness, and unity.

- It helps create in us a love of righteousness, a heightened sense of sin, and a turning away from known evil.

Remember this, as King David encouraged himself in Psalm 56:9-13: "When I cry unto Thee, then shall mine enemies turn back: this I know; for God is for me. In God, will I praise His Word: in the Lord, will I praise His Word. In God have I put my trust: I will not be afraid; what man can do unto me? Thy vows are upon me, O God: I will render praises unto Thee. For thou hast delivered my soul from death: Wilt not thou deliver my feet from falling, that I may walk before God in the light of the living?"

CHAPTER TWELVE

A Prophet Without Honor

"Understanding And Learning The Process Of Honor"

"A prophet is not without honor except in his native place and among his own kin and in his own house (Mark 6:4)." What constitutes success for a prophet? Is it prestigious connections or material possessions or fame? Most prophets have their idea about all three. There are a growing number of maturing prophets who know from experience that status, money and celebrity are no guarantees of happiness and peace.

Ezekiel, Elijah, Jeremiah and other prominent prophets had their apparent lack of success and genuine success according to the standards of their own time and place. Each was a rejected prophet who faced opposition from those who, at least in retrospect, should have accepted and honored them.

In Luke 4:20-30 Jesus' rejection in his own hometown holds two important lessons for prophets. Jesus, fresh from a preaching and healing campaign in Galilee, has returned to Nazareth after an absence of many months. He left a commoner, he returned a celebrity.

On the Sabbath he is invited to read from the sacred scrolls and comment on the text. Nazareth would see what kind of teacher he had become. Jesus reads from Isaiah 61: 1-5, about the Spirit of the Lord anointing him to preach good news, heal and set free, and then says, "Today this scripture has been fulfilled in your hearing" (4:21).

The reaction in the synagogue that Sabbath was one of astonishment. Luke says they were "amazed at the gracious words that came from his lips." The word "amazed" is Greek thaumazo[8], 'wonder, marvel, be astonished' (the context determines whether in a good or bad sense). Apparently they had never heard Jesus as a public speaker or as a teacher. His life among them had been as a carpenter. never a public figure. This was an entirely new role, and they were, as Matthew and Mark put it "astonished," Greek ekplesso[9], "be amazed, overwhelmed" (Matthew 13:54; Mark 6:2) Jesus "gracious words" were impressive.

But was this the astonishment of appreciation or of skepticism? At first glance, we're not sure. The NIV translates verse 22a as, "All spoke well of him..." The word "spoke" is the imperfect tense of the Greek word martureo[10], "la. 'bear witness, be a witness,' b. 'bear witness to, declare, confirm,' 'testify favorably, speak well (of), approve (of)."[3] The word can also be used in the sense " 'to bear witness against,' i.e. 'to condemn.' "[4] Perhaps there was a wave of approval, followed by muttering, "Is not this Joseph's son?"

The congregation's quickness to pigeonhole Jesus as Joseph's son shows that within their spectrum they were unable to view Jesus in any other context that as a member of a Nazareth family. Does this sound familiar to you? They may have been thinking of the scandalous events surrounding his birth. After all, this was a small town, and people talk. Matthew and Mark record other comments of the crowd'

"Where did this man get this wisdom and these miraculous powers?" they asked. "Isn't this the carpenter's son? Isn't his mother's name Mary, and aren't his brothers James, Joseph, Simon and Judas? Aren't all his sisters with us? Where then did this man get all these things?" (Matthew 13:54-56)

They were amazed but skeptical. Remember, these are hometown folks. Sure, he was good with words, but how could he really be worthy of the acclaim and adulation he had been met with elsewhere in Galilee? The congregation "took offense at him." (Matthew 13:57; Mark 6:3)

Jesus sensed the unbelief and skepticism in the room that day. The congregation made no attempt to hide their feelings. Jesus' next comments confront this anti-faith.

"Surely you will quote this proverb to me: 'Physician, heal yourself! Do here in your country what we have heard that you did in Capernaum.' I tell you the truth," he continued, "no prophet is accepted in his hometown." (Luke 4:23-24)

"Physician, heal yourself'" is plain enough. The townspeople are to apply the words to Jesus hometown vs. other towns where Jesus had performed healings. They are simply saying that you've healed elsewhere; how about in your own hometown? The skepticism in Nazareth was so pervasive that Mark records, "He could not do any miracles there, except lay his hands on a few sick people and heal them. And he was amazed at their lack of faith." (Mark 6:5-6)

Jesus' clear implication was that the Israelites in these area-were unworthy of these miracles and so God bestowed miracles on outsiders who believed. It was their actions and commentary about the faith of Jesus as they perceived in Nazareth. Outside this village Jesus had performed amazing miracles, but the unbelief in Nazareth was too thick. Even though they wanted to see a miracle show, they were neither worthy nor ready. A prophet wasn›t honored in his own hometown.

The resentment and skepticism that seethed beneath the surface, now erupted in anger and murder. Luke 4:29-31 shows us that the congregation rose from their Sabbath synagogue worship with intent to kill their homegrown Teacher. They drove Jesus out of the building and out the village. "Drove" or "thrust" is a violent word that means " 'drive out, expel,' literally 'throw out' more or less forcibly, the phrase "took him to the brow of the hill" to" lead away, take into custody, arrest." as well as "of transport of a prisoner, or conducting a condemned man to execution."

Nazareth was built at the edge of a mountain. To the west the ground drops very rapidly to the fertile Jezreel Valley below. Without hearing or trial, and in violation of both Jewish and Roman law, his townspeople intended to kill him by throwing him over a precipice perhaps as a prelude to stoning.

Was Jesus justified in his judgment of their worthiness, faith, and character? Obviously. Though they forced him to the cliff, they couldn't throw him over. Jesus just walked away, through the crowd, and out of town, never to return to his hometown. This was a lesson for us to learn as prophet!

Have you ever wondered why your family, and even some people who know you don't accept your faith or accept you as a prophet? They "know you too well." They remember your past, perhaps, and don't believe you've changed. Though Jesus' family finally came around, the townspeople never did. Sometimes faith means lonely life. A, prophet will know this all too well.

In response his towns people open skepticism, Jesus refers two-stories of how God blessed two non-Jewish individuals, at a time that many Jews had needs that went unmet.

Jesus tells of the widow at Zaraphath, a village on the coast of present-day Lebanon, near Sidon (1 Kings 17:7 24). The Prophet Elijah had stayed with her and her son during the 3.5 year drought that preceded his victory over the prophets of Baal on Mount Carmel. The widow's small jar of flour and tiny jug of oil were not depleted, though they fed the three of them for years. Later, when the widow's son died, Elijah's prayers revived him from the dead. No Israelites received such a blessing.

Then Jesus told of Naaman, general of the army of Israel's enemy Aram, whose capital was Damascus (2 Kings 5). Naaman had leprosy and heard that the Prophet Elisha in Israel had the power to heal. At Elisha's word, Naaman had dipped seven times in the Jordan, and after the seventh time his leprosy was healed and his skin restored like that of a child, There were many lepers in Israel at the time, commented Jesus, but only the foreigner Naaman was healed.

THERE ARE TWO LESSONS PROPHETS NEED TO KNOW:

1. Rejection is part of following Jesus, especially for a prophet. Sometimes we believe that if we witness flawlessly or live perfectly, everyone will like us. Not so. If they rejected Jesus, we can expect to be rejected sometimes, too. Stop second-guessing yourself so much. Instead of focusing on what others think, seek to follow the Lord, not to impress people but for wisdom. Let the chips fall where they may.

2. Rejection is likely to come from those closest to us. By God's grace some of us see our families won to Christ by our testimony, but many don't. A prophet still has no honor in his own country. A stranger would have more belief in you than your own family because they have known you since birth. Jesus couldn't teach His own family because their idea of a king was totally different than what Jesus taught. They thought that His teachings had nothing to do with running a kingdom.

"He was in the world, and though the world was made through him, the world did not recognize him. He came to that which was his own, but his own did not receive him. Yet to all who received him, to those who believed in his name, he gave the right to become children of God." (John 1:10-12)

Some prophets say "Lord, you know how I hate rejection. How I go way out of my way to avoid being or feeling rejected. Help me to grow out of it." As prophets, we need to pray for God to give us courage to face those who distrust, dislike, or resent us for whatever reasons. There are those who look down on you, who think they have you figured out. Ask God to help you to love them while refusing to compromise your integrity. Ask God to forgive you where you've been afraid.

Jesus' public ministry teaches us two things: 1) prophets often suffer opposition from their own people (the rejected prophet), and Jesus stands in the tradition of the prophets Elijah and Elisha (who ministered to non-Jews also), and 2) prophets must be able and willing to minister to everyone!

Around his hometown folks, the problem may well have been the people's feeling that Jesus was not doing enough healing's and other miracles in Nazareth. They may have wanted to keep Jesus for themselves and benefit more from his powers.

Jeremiah 1 shows us that prophets are seldom popular. Prophets tell hard truths and make people confront unpleasant realities. Prophets do not hire pollsters or commission focus groups or depend on social media to validate them.

Their power and authority come from God, not from popular opinion. It is generally true that real prophets seldom find acceptance among their own. This proverb was true of Jeremiah in Jerusalem and of Jesus in Nazareth.

The prophets Elijah and Elisha prefigured the ministry of Jesus in many respects. Those two prophets from the ninth and eighth centuries B.C. taught through parables and symbolic actions, healed the sick and restored dead persons to life, and they suffered rejection and persecution for proclaiming God's will and judgment.

The examples from 1 Kings 17 and 2 Kings 5 showed Elijah and Elisha worked miracles for persons from outside their home areas and even outside the boundaries of Israel.

A recurrent theme among prophets is that, "now that I have shared I will be rejected". It is true that sometimes the word of God will be rejected. That happens independent of the means of transmittal, whether by prophetic word, vision, scripture, sermon, dream or whatever. The Holy Spirit can use many means to bring people to conviction and repentance - even an earthquake (Acts 16: 29-30)!

Sometimes the rejection of the prophet is caused by the manner of the prophet himself or herself if you share a prophecy out of a heart of manipulation or control. People will generally sense that and react against it.

Do you know a prophet or person who left a church or ministry to start up another one, but not without sharing a "word from the Lord" to several key people that the Lord wanted them to join him? The mature who know the prophet or person concerned, can and will reject that message and see it as a rejection of that prophets or that leader's actions based simply on how they conducted themselves, which was without honor. Honor shows itself always with character and today, in the body of Christ, these qualities are so lacking that that's why we see so much rejection constantly. This is sad to the point that so few prophets of this now generation want to accept this type of responsibility in order to learn and grow.

You need to know that if a prophet shares a message out of pride in their abilities as a prophet, or out of anger or anything else that is not totally of God, then that too will be sensed by the recipients and may be rejected, as well as the prophet also.

"The man who enters by the gate is the shepherd of his sheep. The watchman opens the gate for him, and the sheep listen to his voice. He calls his own sheep by name and leads them out. When he has brought out all his own, he goes on ahead of them, and his sheep follow him because they know his voice. But they will never follow a stranger; in fact, they will run away from him because they do not recognize a stranger's voice." (John 10:3-5)

Let's consider if as a prophet our words are rejected. Ask the fundamental question: "To the best of my knowledge, having asked the Holy Spirit to shed His light on my conscience, did I share God's word in God's way at God's time to God's choice of audience?"

If the answer to that question is not a certain "yes", then there is an element of my own responsibility for the rejection of the word. I can't just blame other people "stubbornly" rejecting the word of the Kord.

One of the classic tricks of the enemy is to cause a prophet to feel alienated from the rest of the flock, like Elijah in 1 King 19:14. There may often even be some justification for the sense of hurt.

It is critical and important for the prophet or prophetess to keep his or her eyes on the Lord. Only He can direct us what to do in these type circumstances. Only He can heal the wounds of rejection. Sometimes a "wedge» or distance is formed in the prophet›s heart between the prophet. and the people he or she have been sent to serve.

Having a wedge in your heart is not the heart of Jesus, who is intimately and passionately in love with His flock and who fully identifies with us even to the point of taking our sin upon

Himself at Calvary. This difference between the heart of the prophet and the heart of the Good Shepherd will become evident sooner or later to those whom you are sent to serve, and sometimes people will in turn run away from you simply because you are a prophet.

Prophets have always played a very important part in the unfolding of the plan and purpose of God. Prophets, you are front line soldiers in the army of the Lord and that's the plan of God. Prepare yourself for the mission of your calling and understand God's process for your development.

CHAPTER THIRTEEN

The Face To Face Anointing

THE LIFE VISION OF MOSES

"Are You Willing To Do What It Takes?"

For all aspiring Prophetic Eagles in God, the story of Moses is an excellent role model for all of us to study and learn from. The story of Moses is the blueprint of the individual prophetic journey with the Lord. Talk about being in the wilderness.

In Exodus 2, we see Moses' mother attempting to save her child by placing him in a basket and putting it into the Nile. The basket was eventually found by pharaoh's daughter, and she adopts him as her own and raises him in the palace of the pharaoh himself. As Moses grows into adulthood, he begins to empathize with the plight of his people, and upon witnessing an Egyptian beating a Hebrew slave, Moses intervenes and kills the Egyptian.

In another incident, Moses attempts to intervene in a dispute between two Hebrews, but one of the Hebrews rebukes Moses and sarcastically comments, "Are you going to kill me as you did the Egyptian?" (Exodus 2:14) Realizing that his criminal act was made known, Moses flees to the land of Midian where he again plays the hero this time to the daughters of Jethro by rescuing them from some bandits. In gratitude, Jethro grants the hand of his daughter Zipporah to Moses.

The next major incident in Moses' life is his encounter with God at the burning bush in Exodus 3, where God calls Moses to be the savior of His people. Moses needed time to grow, mature and learn to be meek and humble before God. This brings us to the next chapter in Moses' life, his 40 years in the land of Midian. During this time, Moses learned the simple life of a shepherd, a husband, and a father. God took an impulsive and hot-tempered young man and began the process of molding and shaping him into the perfect instrument for God to use.

What can we learn from this time in his life? If the first lesson is to wait on God's timing, the second lesson is to not be idle

while we wait on God's timing. While the Bible doesn't spend a
lot of time on the details of this part of Moses' life, it's not as if
Moses was sitting idly by waiting for God's call.

He spent the better part of 40 years learning the ins and
outs of being a shepherd and supporting and raising a family. These are not trivial things! While we might long for the
"mountain top" experiences with God, 99 percent of our lives
are lived in the valley doing the mundane, day-to-day things
that make up a life. We need to be living for God "in the valley"
before He will enlist us into the battle. What will it take for us
as prophets to understand this? Like Moses, we are in the wilderness for a reason. His reason was to be prepared as is ours.

Another thing we see from Moses during his time spent in
Midian is that, when God finally did call him into service, Moses
was resistant. The man of action early in his life, in his early
40's is , now 80 years old. Moses is somewhat overly timid. When
called to speak for God, Moses said he was "slow of speech and
tongue." Moses had a stuttering issue with his speech. Let's
learn from the great Moses!

Moses shows us what a prophets personal relationship with
God should be like. The number one thing God wants with each
prophet is to establish a close, intimate, personal relationship.
Moses definitely accomplished this with God the Father! The
Face to Face Anointing represents finest and highest compli-
ments that any person could ever hope to receive from God
Himself. Here are the two verses giving Moses these two incred-
ible compliments direct from the Lord Himself:

"So the Lord spoke to Moses face to face, as a man speaks to his friend." Exodus 33:11 Also look at this - Deuteronomy 34:10 says "But since then there has not arisen in Israel a prophet like Moses, whom the Lord knew face to face." When God first manifested His presence up on top of Mount Sinai, all the other Israelites were scared to death of God. The people told Moses that he should go up there and talk with God for them lest they should die from coming into direct contact with the Lord.

Moses was a man of action that the people knew; he had a special relationship with God. The Face to Face Anointing is a relationship of The Anointing in Action. As a Prophet you want this! Do you really have a special relationship with God? When God first makes contact with Moses, He tells Moses that He has chosen him to go into Egypt to deliver the children of Israel from their plight with the Egyptians.

Moses then starts to argue with God, asking who is he to accomplish such a mission. He reminded Him, that he is too slow of speech and tongue, and for God to consider asking someone else to do this for Him.

God then replies back to Moses that he has nothing to worry about, that He will be with him, and that He will be with his mouth and teach him what to say. In other words, God was telling Moses that His anointing would be on him to accomplish this incredible or what looks like impossible task. Imagine his thoughts of what type of action it would take on his part to accomplish what seemed to be impossible.

We see that Moses life changed for the better, and what an incredible adventure he had with God in the last 40 years of his life! Moses was 80 years old when God first made contact with him and called him out for the deliverance mission that He had in store for him. Everything that Moses experienced in the Lord all occurred in the last 40 years of his life. You never know what God may do with the rest of what time you have left down here on this earth! We must stop underestimating situations just because they look a certain way.

Moses did two powerful things that dramatically changed the course and quality of his life:

1. He entered into and followed God's personal call on his life.
2. He entered into a good, intimate, personal relationship with God.

All Prophets need to realize that if God calls you to do anything on His behalf, He will also anoint you with His supernatural power to get the job done. We all have the Holy Spirit living and dwelling on the inside of us. The Anointing of God is the presence and power of the Holy Spirit operating through us as prophets of God to accomplish whatever, God asks us to do for Him.

The story of Moses is a dramatic example of the "anointing in action" operating through an individual to accomplish what appeared to be an impossible mission, that became possible when Moses stepped out and entered into God's power and anointing!

He literally accomplished the impossible through the power of God, changing the entire course of Jewish history as a result! The odds were totally against Moses accomplishing such a task! However, the Bible says that nothing is impossible with God the Father. Without any shadow of a doubt, God's supernatural power can overcome any situation—no matter how hopeless it may look to you in the natural.

Prophets for those of you who are ever faced with what appears to be an impossible mission or task to perform, just remember Moses story and what happened when he was willing to step out with enough belief and faith in God to let His supernatural power flow and operate through him. He literally changed the entire course of Jewish history with the deliverance of the Israelites from the Egyptians. If God did all of this for Moses, what can He do for his other Prophets? God has no respect of person.

Finally I want to explore the concept that The Bible says that God "knew" (Deuteronomy 34:10) or "spoke to Moses face to face." (Exodus 33:11). Looking at Numbers 12. Aaron and Miriam had spoken against Moses and arrogantly asked: "Has the Lord indeed spoken only through Moses? Has He not spoken through us also?" (Numbers 12:2) God then appeared to Aaron and Miriam, saying: "If there is a prophet among you, I, the Lord, make Myself known to him in a vision; I speak to him in a dream. Not so with My servant Moses; He is faithful in all My house. I speak with him face to face, even plainly, and not in dark sayings; and he sees the form of the Lord" (Numbers 12:6-8).

God spoke to the prophets of Israel through visions and dreams, but to Moses He spoke, "not in dark sayings," but "plainly." In other words, God, who never showed His face to Moses (Exodus 33:20), nevertheless allowed Moses to see "some unmistakable evidence of His glorious presence" and spoke to him "face to face, as a man speaks to his friend" (33:11), i.e., He spoke to Moses plainly, directly, etc. This is an honor above all honors.

The Holy Spirit is teaching us how we as prophets can have the same face-to-face relationship (Anointing of Action) with the Almighty. We have this amazing example of how we should be praying. "If I have found grace in thy sight, show me now thy way, that I may know thee." (Exodus 33:13) Don't be afraid to ask God.

We have been told that we have found grace in his sight and most of us have this as our basic doctrine for salvation. Satisfaction of this knowledge alone is not the grace that is intended for us but unless we hunger and thirst for this grace to be revealed we cannot truly know God. We as prophets must hunger for his presence.

Without a full heart felt desire and a genuine pursuit of this grace that is promised, we cannot boast of faith, and faith without works is dead. Faith in a doctrine does not bring life-changing grace. It's not what you believe that is so important as who you believe. Do you believe God? If you believe the promise of him who cannot lie you will live with full expectation of this grace and it will bring the life giving change, that is desired.

Moses insisted that the presence of God go with him, and the grace of God is nothing less than the presence of God. Only in his presence can the grace of God be found. The mere knowledge of grace does not bring grace, but the pursuit of his presence will. Moses' desired to see the glory of God, God was pleased with his request and he was told "I will make all my goodness pass before thee." Moses was also told, "thou canst not see my face: for there shall no man see me, and live."

Moses was told, "there is a place by me, and thou shalt stand upon a rock: And it shall come to pass, while my glory passeth by, that I will put thee in a clift of the rock, and will cover thee with my hand while I pass by: And I will take away mine hand, and thou shalt see my back parts: but my face shall not be seen."

Prophet, did you consider that Moses was not afraid of the Manifest Presence of God? Not only was Moses not afraid to enter into a close, intimate, personal relationship with God, but he also was not afraid of the manifest presence of God. Today if we will be honest with ourselves, we will see that some prophets really seem to be afraid of any kind of direct contact with God.

Understand this: once you have had any kind of direct, supernatural activity from the Lord, you will know that there is absolutely nothing to be afraid of in reference to the manifestations that we have all received as prophets.

Moses stayed true, loyal, and faithful to God the Father during the entire 40-year journey in the wilderness. The Israelites were constantly complaining, moaning, and bellyaching about their lot. Not enough food, not enough water, not enough this, not enough that. The reality is they lacked for nothing. God made sure they had enough manna raining down from heaven on a daily basis to keep them properly fed.

They also had no problems with God providing adequate shelter and protection for them. Still this was not enough. It seems strange that every Israelite man 20 years and older did not make it into the Promised Land due to their lack of faith in the Lord and failing to follow Him fully. Thus Moses was constantly surrounded by negativity and pessimism with all of these people surrounding him. Prophets does this remind you of your life? And yet Moses never got tired of talking about God and making sure that all of God's laws and commandments were known.

Negativity and pessimism can be contagious, but it never affected Moses. He stayed true, loyal, and faithful to the Lord during these trying times, and he never once strayed from God as His loyal representative. What an example for us to learn from. There is no doubt his experience in the wilderness prepared him.

The Anointing of Action is an Anointing of Change also. Moses got God to change His mind! When Moses was up on Mount Sinai for 40 days and 40 nights with God the Father getting the 10 commandments, the Israelites were down at the bottom of the mountain making a false idol by way of a golden calf.

God sees this, and becomes so furious that He literally wants to consume the Israelites right there on the spot.

Moses sees how mad God is getting and what He is wanting to do to these people, and he immediately "steps into the gap" as he pleaded with the Lord his God, and said:

"Lord, why does Your wrath burn hot against Your people whom you have brought out of the land of Egypt with great power and with a mighty hand?

Why should the Egyptians speak, and say, 'He brought them out to harm them, to kill them in the mountains, and to consume them from the face of the earth?'

Turn from Your fierce wrath and relent from this harm to Your people. Remember Abraham, Isaac, and Israel, your servants, to whom You swore by Your own self, and said to them, 'I will multiply your descendants as the stars of heaven; and all this land that I have spoken of I give to your descendants, and they shall inherit it forever." "So the Lord relented from the harm which He said He would do to His people (Exodus 32:11-14)." Moses qualifies for intense study as we see and understand this anointing of action and change.

Every prophet needs to see what Moses did. There is power in intercessory prayer, and God will turn a situation around if we approach God properly. God can be moved to answer prayer, especially prayers that come from the heart. Standing in the gap means you personally stand in the gap for someone else. You are praying to God for someone else. The power of intercessory prayer.

Sometimes people may be too weak to pray for themselves. Other times some people are either not saved or they have no real personal relationship established with God and are not confident enough to get God to answer their personal prayers. There could be many reasons as to why you would have to stand in the gap for someone else and go to God and ask Him to do something specific for that other person.

There are other Scripture verses that say we can approach God to reason with Him, to state our case before Him. This means God can be talked to, reasoned with, pleaded with, and sometimes persuaded to change His mind on something. Moses is a very good role model and example on how to go into intercession.

God will lead you on a daily basis and if God did all of this for Moses, then He will do it for each and every prophet who will fully surrender their lives over to Him and are willing to be led by the Holy Spirit on a daily basis. God will anoint and empower you and perfectly lead you every step of the way if you are willing to take this journey with Him. God's "power" and "leadings" are ready and waiting for each and every prophets who will fully surrender their lives over to Him.

Moses story proves that God can and will take each of his Prophets on their own individual, unique, and exciting journey with Him if they would only be willing to take that leap of faith and fully surrender their entire lives over to Him. God will fight battles for you when needed. You don't know, the extreme lengths to which God will go for you if He is forced to fight and engage with any enemy standing in your way.

God was wanting His people delivered from their slavery to the Egyptians and He was not going to take no for an answer. God threw ten powerful judgments at the Pharaoh in order to break him so that he would let His people go. Finally, after breaking on the last judgment, the Pharaoh agrees to let God's people go.

However, after initially letting them go, the Pharaoh all of a sudden changed his mind and started to go after them. The Israelites got caught before the Red Sea. God parted the Red Sea with a dry ground mass so they could safely cross over to the other side.

Prophets, if you have been at the end of a cliff needing a major miracle from God to save you, then you know it is not something that you should ever want to experience. It is scary, nerve wracking, and it will test your patience and faith in God to its absolute limits like it did with Moses and the Israelites. The Israelites started complaining once they got caught up in this situation. But Moses, whose faith and confidence in God had been built up during the time God was manifesting His ten judgments on the Pharaoh, stepped forward and boldly proclaimed that God was going to save the day for them and that He would deliver them from the predicament they now found themselves caught up in.

If any of you should ever find yourself before your own personal red sea with nowhere else to go, then remember what God did for Moses. No matter how bleak or how hopeless the situation may appear to you in the natural, remember that nothing is impossible with our God! If God can literally part the Red Sea like He did in this story with Moses, then God can part and take care of your red sea if you are willing to press in, request that He help you out, and be willing to believe and have faith that He will take care of the situation.

We as prophets must go through The Wilderness Experience like Moses did to test you, to see if you have what it takes to make the grade, to make the call that He has set up for your life. "Many are called, but few are chosen." You should consider yourself chosen as you read this. God has something specific that He wants them to do in your life. He has a mission and a purpose for your lives. Prophets, remember you are in a price-paying period.

The curse of Adam and Eve is still in full operation in this world. There is a price to pay for anything good that we will want in this life. If you want God's prophetic call on your life, then there is going to be some kind of price you are going to have to pay to receive this call. Many of the times this price is actually paid in some type of wilderness experience. Some prophets do not want to pay a price for anything. They want everything handed to them free of charge. These types of prophets will never make it with God in reference to the call that He would like to put on their lives.

It is in the wilderness experience that you will really draw close to God. He will strip out many of the normal things in your life. You feel like you're out in the desert all by yourself and that it is only you and God going through all of this. Your social life may also wane greatly during this time. He also may strip your finances down during this period to just enough to get you by. The reason He is doing this is to see if you will stay faithful and loyal to Him. It is very easy to have faith and belief in God when everything is going good and great, but when things start to go bad, and you start to lose some of your own material possessions, then the real test will come into play.

Will you stay true, loyal, and faithful to God during these lean and dry times, or will you bail out on Him because the going is getting too tough? Many prophets do not make it through this tough time of testing, and they then end up missing out on their calls with God. God wants the same thing from each of us. The wilderness experience will really cause this kind of grafting to take place with you and the Lord.

This kind of experience will usually make or break you in your own personal relationship with God. If you make it all the way through and allow this grafting to occur, you will then become much closer to God in your own personal relationship with Him.

Do Not Always Be Questioning God. There is a time to question God, to press in and seek after answers from Him. The Bible says to ask, and you shall receive. Seek, and you will find. However, there is also a time not to question God and to accept whatever He is telling you to do!

When God first makes contact with Moses through the burning bush, He tells Moses exactly what He wants him to do. He tells Moses that He will use him to deliver the children of Israel out from under their bondage to the Egyptians.

During this initial conversation with God, Moses questions God's wisdom of choosing him for the job! Moses asks who he is to accomplish such a task. He says he is too slow of speech and tongue, and then he finally tells God to consider calling someone else for the job. The Bible says that Moses ended up kindling the anger of God with the pessimism that he was showing to God.

God finally gives in at this point and tells Moses that He will also anoint his brother Aaron for the job, that He will be with the both of them, and that Aaron will be his mouthpiece to the people since Moses had no faith in God's anointing to enable him to speak effectively to the people and to the Pharaoh. When God calls you and ask you to do something specific, do not ever question His wisdom on the matter. God's knowledge and ways are absolutely perfect. Even if you do not think that you have what it takes to accomplish what He is asking you to do, remember that His anointing and power will be on you to enable you to accomplish that task or mission!

His supernatural power flowing through you will be more than enough to successfully accomplish whatever He will be asking you to do for Him. The story of Moses is a perfect, dramatic, and powerful example of just how far someone can go with God if they are willing to follow God fully and not be afraid to walk with His anointing. Do Not Disobey a Direct Order From God.

The saddest part of Moses life is that he was not allowed to go into the Promised Land because of one act of disobedience. God had given him a direct order to speak out to a rock and God would then cause water to flow out from this rock. For some strange reason, Moses ends up striking the rock twice with his rod instead of speaking out direct to it as God had specifically commanded him to do.

Moses had disobeyed a direct order from God on how to perform this miracle. As a result, God kept him from going into the Promised Land, and he died out in the wilderness. Some people may wonder why God was so harsh with Moses on this particular matter. Moses had done just about everything else right in God.

Why would God hold this one particular act against him? God was holding Moses to a much higher standard as he does with his prophets. To whom much is given, much more will be expected!

Moses was also dealing with a miracle that God wanted to perform. When you get into this level with God where He is manifesting miracles through you, this demands strict and perfect obedience to God. There is no negotiating with God in this higher level with Him.

If God wants to manifest a particular miracle through you, then you better do exactly what God says as to how He wants to bring the miracle or manifestation about. This is one area where you cannot question God or attempt to try to do it your own way. If you do, you could seriously jeopardize anything else that God may want to do through you. You could lose your call, your ministry, your anointing, and any other blessings that God may have in store for you.

For those of you who will ever receive any kind of direct order from God on any issue—do not disobey the order or try to do it your own way like Moses did. If you do, the consequences could be severe. In some cases, it could be a matter of your own life and death. Remember—God always knows best—you do not.

In conclusion of the Face-to-Face Anointing, we see the story of Moses ends up on a rather sad note with him not being able to enter into the Promised Land. Also we need to look and remember all the good things that he did right in God. His resume is impressive, but we learn the Face-to-Face Anointing is birthed through a strict obedience.

- Speaks directly to God through a burning bush.

- Used by God to change the entire course of Jewish history by delivering the Israelites from the Egyptians.

- Watched God throw ten powerful judgments against Egypt.

- Watched God part the Red Sea.

- Personally received The Ten Commandments from God the Father.

- Talked a second time with God the Father up on Mt. Sinai.

- Saw the manifested presence of God with God showing him His back side up on Mt. Sinai.

- Watched God's manifested presence come down on the tabernacle they had built and lead them on a daily basis.

- Be directly responsible for the teaching of God and all of His ways to the younger generation of Israelites who eventually would be the ones to enter into the Promised Land.

CHAPTER FOURTEEN

Angels And Prophets

"The Awesome Relationship of God's Word in Action"

Many prophets simply do not adhere or believe in essence of angelic assistance in their everyday walk and assignments. Gods angelic army helps us operate in God's law of blessing, abundance, and breakthrough. Angels are a creation of God. They are purely spiritual and splendid beings that require no food, drink or sleep. They have no physical desires or material needs. Like other creations of God, angels spend their time worshiping God. In contrast to human beings, Angels do not have free will. They can only obey God and do not have the ability to disobey Him. Each Angel is charged with a certain duty. Angels cannot be seen by the naked eyes.

It's a fine line between an angel's task and the task of a prophet, or anyone who brings us a word from God that we really don't want to hear. There is abundant mention of angels in the Bible. The nature of this revelation is without the same kind of explicit description we often find with other subjects developed in Scripture: every reference to angels is incidental to some other topic. God's revelation never aims at informing us regarding the nature of angels. When they are mentioned, it is always to inform us further about God, what he does, and how he does it.

Angels are spirit beings (Hebrews 1:14) which were created by God (Genesis 2:1 and Colossians 1:16). Exactly when they were created is not clear, but they pre-date the creation of the material universe because the scriptures say that they witnessed the creation and rejoiced over it (Job 38:4-7). The very word, angel, is derived from the Greek word, angelos[11], which means "messenger." The Hebrew equivalent, malakh[12], also means "messenger."

The manifestation of the gifts of the Holy Spirit are a sign from God. As prophets, angels are ministering for us as we operate in these gifts. When a person is slain in the spirit it can feel like someone physically pushed you down or clipped you behind the knees. It's an angel of the Lord that is doing the work of the Holy Spirit.

Some prophets demonstrate more of the gifts in their ministry than others. Have you ever wondered why? The reason is that some have more angels appointed to them than some of the other prophets. As you continue to minister as a prophet you begin to recognize the different presence of the various angels at work in your ministry.

This is one way how we know what gift the Holy Spirit will have you to operate in next. The presence of the ministering spirit that slays people in the Holy Ghost is different from that of the ministering spirit that brings the gift of healings.

There are various gifts and ministry functions imparted by God appointed to different prophets. This is why empowerment is critical. This is so God can use us in any situation he chooses to put us in. Situations like the gift of healings; not healing but HEALINGS. It is plural.

"And God has appointed these in the church: first apostles, second prophets, third teachers, after that miracles, then gifts of healings, helps, administrations, varieties of tongues" (I Corinthians 12:28). There are angels that have different powers over disease and sickness, just as Gabriel has different powers than Michael.

Some prophets will struggle and get frustrated and turn from using the gift God has given them. There are times they will pray for the sick and they would be healed and other times they would not. Out of frustration they gave it up all together. Prophet, you must learn that you will never perfect the gift by using it until you understand the measure of its power. The angel is there to enforce the covenant of God as you use your prophetic gift.

We perfect the gift by using it and understanding the measure of its power. When a prophet comes into understanding the power of the angelic host have that is appointed to you, you will start to mature in your gift and accuracy becomes clear and consistent.

To experience the accuracy of your prophetic gift, you must first find out what your specific calling is. When you know your calling and begin following its course then you can focus on your gift. Many of our today's prophets seem to just want to identify with their gift, but do not have a clue as to what their calling is. If you do not follow your calling, your angel is not obligated to minister for you, hence no manifestation of the gifts.

Your prophetic calling may have a specialty of prophetic evangelism, prophetic teaching faith, hearing God, feeding the poor, or helping less fortunate. Prophet, whatever you are called of God to do, God is faithful to endorse it by signs and wonders following you. However, if we are not willing to do what God has called you to do, He is not bound to send His Angels to minister for you. Once you have clarity of what your calling is, then do it.

Hebrews 1:13-14 says, "Sit at My right hand, Till I make Your enemies Your footstool?" "Are they not all ministering spirits sent forth to minister for those who will inherit salvation?" When dealing with the prophetic, angels are a vital part in seeing the word delivered with power. Angels are sent to signoff and clarify what God's purpose is for His people and for the lost. Angels are never given the responsibility of proclaiming the Gospel. This is the work of the Holy Spirit through humans such as the five-fold ministry such as the prophet, angels are often portrayed as playing an active role in ministry preparation.

"Do not forget to show hospitality to strangers, for by so doing some people have shown hospitality to angels without knowing it" (Hebrews 13:2). Angels are still among us. Their very name means "messenger" and we can be assured that when they are here, they have come for a certain purpose. For they have been sent by God.

5 BASIC REASONS GOD SENDS ANGEL TO PROPHETS:

1.TO GIVE A MESSAGE FROM GOD

There are many examples in the Bible of when God sends an angel to give a specific message to an individual or people. In Genesis 18, God sent three men, messengers, to Abraham, the first prophet and Sarah to tell them that she would bear a son. He sent an angel to Sarah's servant Hagar in the desert, as she fled in Genesis 16, to give hope that she was not forgotten.

2. TO PROTECT US

Many times God sends angels to protect, guard, and fight for us. God tells us in Psalm 91 that He would give angels charge concerning us to guard us in all our ways.

God sent an angel to Daniel in the lion's den. Daniel 6:22 says
that he shut the mouth of the lions so that no harm came to him
who was found blameless before God. Psalm 34:7 reminds us,
"The angel of the Lord encamps around those who fear him, and
delivers them." In 2 Kings 6:17, Elisha prayed that his servant
would see the armies of angels surrounding the city. God opened
his eyes, and he realized he had overlooked these mighty invisible beings.

3. TO SERVE BELIEVERS

God sends angels to minister to those who hurt or need
strength. When Elijah was afraid and running for his life in 1
Kings 19, an angel appeared to him and provided food and water
for his journey.

4. TO EXECUTE GOD'S JUDGMENT

Angels can be used by God to punish sin and to bring his
judgment.

5. TO GIVE PRAISE AND WORSHIP TO GOD

Angels are mighty beings of praise and worship unto
God. Revelation 4:8 says, "Day and night they never stop saying,
'Holy, holy, holy is the Lord God Almighty, who was, and is, and
is to come.'"

The book of Revelation was given to John by an angel. No Prophets of God can deny that God gave the angel to Him to show His servants; things which must shortly take place. And He sent and signified it by His angel to His servant John, who bore witness to the word of God, and to the testimony of Jesus Christ, to all things that he saw. Blessed is he who reads and those who hear the words of this prophecy and keep those things which are written in it; for the time is near (Revelation 1:1-3)."

"Then he (the angel) said to me, "These words are faithful and true." And the Lord God of the holy prophets sent His angel to show His servants the things which must shortly take place (Revelation 22:6)."

"I, Jesus have sent My angel to testify to you these things in the churches. I am the Root and the Offspring of David, the Bright and Morning Star (Revelation 22:16).". The reality of angels is that they will take on human form to minister to those who are in the process of spiritual growth (Hebrews 1:14)."

When the prophet gets the Word in them the angels will be waiting with great anticipation for the prophets to begin prophesying the words that were sent to them. Until the prophets speak the Word on earth as it has been declared in heaven, the angels of God cannot do anything. They lay in wait for the hour, the day, the month and the year to be released by the word of the prophets.

When the angels of the Lord come bringing the word of God in the form that the prophets can digest and understand, only then will they know the will of God and what needs to be spoken on earth in accordance with His Word in heaven.

"Then I took the little book out of the angel's hand and ate it, and it was as sweet as honey in my mouth. But when I had eaten it, my stomach became bitter. And he said to me, 'You must prophesy again about many peoples, nations, tongues, and kings' (Revelation 10:10,11)."

After the prophets have the knowledge that they received from the angels, the angels will start pleading with the prophets to prophesy the words that were written in the little book that they ate. You see, the angels cannot begin the war until the prophet's start prophesying that which God has declared. So what are the things these prophets will be prophesying?

The prophetic actions of the prophet are critical as the angels are sent to help transition prophets to their next levels in the anointing. Many prophets simply ignore the angels, because they don't understand they are there to help with the transition assignment for them and, therefore, the prophet fails to ascend. To many prophets are working in their own strength, and struggling and failing to embrace the work of My angels on assignment to help them transition. Prophets God is sending angels in times of transition." Only God can transition you from glory to glory, but there are angels to help you.

"Then he lay down under the bush and fell asleep. All at once an angel touched him and said Get up and eat (1 Kings 19:5)"

The prophet Elijah is being fed by the angel in his transition as a mentor to a future prophet to the Nations named Elisha.

It was an angel spoke to Moses sternly about angelic protection in Exodus 23:20-22: "Indeed, I am going to send an angel before you to guard you along the way and to bring you into the place which I have prepared. Be on guard before him and obey his voice. Do not provoke him, for he will not pardon your transgressions, for My name is in him. But if you diligently obey his voice and do all that I say, then I will be an enemy to your enemies and an adversary to your adversaries."

Psalm 103:20 says, "Bless the Lord you His angels, who are mighty, and do His commands, and obey the voice of His word." The Message Bible says, "So bless God, you angels, ready and able to fly at his bidding, quick to hear and do what he says. Bless God, all you armies of angels, alert to respond to whatever he wills.

Jesus spoke of two kinds of angels — the "angels in Heaven" Matthew 22:30 and "the devil and his angels" Matthew 25:41. The latter seem to have originated from Satan's rebellion against God.

Satan was originally one of God's most glorious angels, "full of wisdom and perfect in beauty (Ezekiel 28:12)." But his heart became lifted up because of his beauty Ezekiel 28:17, and his pride motivated him to try to take the throne of God Isaiah 14:12-14. Due to his rebellion, he was cast out of Heaven, down to earth, and one third of the angels were cast out with him because they joined his rebellion Revelation 12:4. These fallen angels are the demons that are referred to in both the Old and New Testaments. Satan, in fact, is called the "ruler of the demons (Matthew 9:34)."

When angels take on human form, they appear like any normal person, as seen in Genesis 18:2 and Genesis 19:1-17. When they manifest themselves in their spirit form, they tend to appear as dazzling light (Matthew 28:1-4).

Angels have emotions. They rejoiced over the creation of the universe Job 38:7, and we are told that "there is joy in the presence of the angels of God over one sinner who repents"(Luke 15:10)."

Angels do not marry or procreate (Matthew 22:30). They do not age nor are they subject to death (Luke 20:36). Therefore, their numbers remain constant. The exact number is not revealed, but Ten thousand angels appeared to Moses on Mount Sinai (Deuteronomy 33:2). David saw 20,000 at one time (Psalm 68:17). When John was raptured to the throne room of God, he saw ten times ten thousand (Revelation 5:11). The book of Hebrews says there are "innumerable myriads (Hebrews 12:22)."

Angels have great knowledge, but they are not omniscient. Jesus said, for example, that angels do not know when His Second Coming will take place (Mark 13:32). They are obedient servants of their Creator (Psalm 103:20).Angels are not gods, and therefore, they are not to be worshiped (Colossians 2:18 ; Revelation 22:8-9). I have seen no biblical passage that says angels have to eat to stay alive, but the Bible portrays them as eating when they take on human form (Genesis 18:1-8;19:1-3). Also, Psalm 78:25 refers to the manna God provided to feed the children of Israel in the wilderness as "the bread of angels." Interesting to say the least, prophets.

The singing of angels is implied in two ways. First, by their words are often expressed in poetic form (Luke 2:14,;Revelation 4:8,11; 5:9-10,12-13). Second, music is a universal form of worship, and angels are pictured worshiping the Lord unceasingly (Psalm 148:1-2 ;Revelation 4-5).When angels speak to a prophet, they will always use that person's native language. The Bible indicates that angels have a language of their own that they use among themselves. Some angels seem to have highly specialized responsibilities that relate to the natural universe. Revelation 16:5 refers to "the angel of the waters." The angel "who has power over fire" is referred in Revelation 14:18. In Revelation 7:1 four angels are pictured who have control of the winds of the earth.

Hebrews 1:14 indicates that believers may have guardian angels: "Are they [angels] not all ministering spirits sent out to render service for the sake of those who will inherit salvation?" which does include us as the prophets of God. A companion verse to Hebrews 1:14 can be found in Psalm 91:11-12 For He will give His angels charge concerning you, to guard you in all your ways. They will bear you up in their hands, lest you strike your foot against a stone.

God gives his messengers charge still today to bring a message of hope, to protect, to serve, to carry out his judgment, and to give him praise. What we can prophets learn from angels?

- We can recognize that angels are real, they are God's messengers, and there is a vast spiritual realm that surrounds us day to day, though we can't visibly see it (Colossians 1:16).

- We do not need to fear angels. Though this may be our normal response if we met one face to face, the Bible reminds us that we do not need to fear (Luke 2:10).

- God never intends for us to worship angels or to pray to them. He alone is worthy of our worship (Revelation 4:11).

- We do not have authority over angels, only God does. The Bible never tells us to give them instruction or to command them (Psalm 91:11).

- We are wise to walk with spiritual discernment, for the Bible says that even the devil himself will disguise himself as an angel of light. We can recognize truth and deception through his Spirit who guides us (2 Corinthians 11:14).

CHAPTER FIFTEEN

Full Time Prophetic Ministry

GOD'S NEXT STEP FOR YOU

"Don't Move Until You Master The Basics"

Prophets are being called into full-time ministry all the time. You might be one of them. Many others have sensed God speaking to them too. Every prophet should remember Samuel's call. In the middle of the night he heard God calling him. He needed Eli to clarify some things for him that put him on the right track. Eli's advice wasn't anything astonishing. He simply told Samuel that when God called again, he was to tell the Lord "Speak, Lord for thy servant heareth."

Prophets of this generation who sense a pull in the heart from the Lord often have many questions. They are searching for answers. They are wondering if they are on the right track. This chapter will move you to an awakening from your wilderness season but your leader should address your personal situation questions. Let's now get you on the right track to find the answers that you need.

God deals with each prophet differently, and yet He brings each willing prophet along a similar pathway. That is the amazing fact. The focus here is to encourage and confirm you on your way. The Lord is the One who both calls and directs your training.

He is the One who gifts us as well as the One who provides for us. It is for these reasons that every genuine prophet of God will have his ear tuned to what God is saying and know its God.

TIMING AND TRAINING IS IMPORTANT

One of the first impulses prophets get is that when we sense God's calling upon our lives, we think we need to make a drastic, radical shift, at that very moment. Although it could happen that way, it doesn't necessarily need to.

Prophets, first God touches our hearts and gains our commitment to His plan for our lives. We then have a great burden to serve the Lord full-time, but we still have a significant amount of training to go through before the Lord deploys us as full-time prophets and apostles. Maybe some of you will want to read this again, but this is a fact we can't overlook.

One of the biggest mistakes of some prophets who have received God's call to enter full time ministry is to think that Bible College or seminary is what qualifies them to serve the Lord. Although a seminary can further equip us in some ways, we do ourselves much harm when we equate this kind of training with the prophetic training that the Lord wants to provide for our lives. Prophets train prophets. This is not a theory, but this is a fact. You will need a prophetic mentor to educate you in the things of the prophetic. Take your time and find a mentor. Sometimes it will take time to understand what you are looking for in a mentor but find one and become a sponge.

Prophet, you also must understand that the Lord sees His equipping of us for service in a broad way. The Lord's training involves each part of our lives. Prophet, you need mentor-ship to understand what God is doing. God is much more interested in building our faith than in any degree we might obtain. There is no disrespect intended here. Different ways for different primary gifts. God is very involved in the process of how He equips prophets for service or spiritual growth for that matter. Prophets are trained through what many of us consider the mundane times of our personal lives.

One of our biggest mistakes Prophets make is to think God is not actively working in life events that seem like long boring night shifts, dealing with personal attacks, attempts to pay off loans, finding a life partner or something trivial like filling out applications.

God uses financial needs, parental objections, lack of opportunity, difficult neighbors, spousal conflict, and the like to further train us. The Lord is in no hurry. If he were, then He would quickly eliminate the obstacles. The mission is urgent and yet, God wants to properly train us because He wants us to succeed.

The Lord will take the time necessary to carry out that training. If God is patient with the training process, then shouldn't we be also? This is not just true for our spiritual lives but also for all the extra challenges and temptations of ministry. Just trace the Apostle Paul's life. The training can even increase at the end of one's ministry! Ok, prophets, now let's look at some practical steps for moving into full time prophetic ministry.

You are emerging in prophetic ministry. You are excited and passionate about your message and the call of God. Intimacy with God is and must be your number one priority.

Most prophets are always asking:

- Why is my ministry not progressing quickly?

- How do I get more opportunities to share my prophetic insights?

- What do I do about the call of God?

1. BE CONFIDENT ABOUT GOD'S CALL. 'THE LORD WILL PERFECT THAT WHICH CONCERNS ME.'

Psalms 138:8 Know that Gods time is not like yours. This is a life changing experience. While you can be intense do not get stressed when various doors of opportunity don't open for you.

Trust God's timing and relax in the call, focusing on faithfulness in stewarding our gifts, as well as serving and honoring leadership. Our role is to position—His role is to promote. He is faithful and will open the doors in His time.

2. BE RELEVANT IN YOUR UTTERANCE. 'AND THE COMMON PEOPLE HEARD HIM GLADLY.' MARK 12:37B

Jesus spoke in the language and expression of the day and shared stories and pictures that people could relate to in their everyday life. Share your prophetic insight; share it in a straightforward way that people understand and can relate to. The prophetic is about receiving a revelation from the Father's heart and then conveying it in such a way that people understand and receive it in the way He intends and is relevant to the people to whom you are ministering to.

3. BE TRUE TO YOURSELF

It's always easy to admire someone else's ministry to emulate them, but frauds will always be exposed when they are copying someone else or trying to be something they are not. Prophetic ministry is not about spiritual formulas, using certain words, style of speech or actions. Prophetic ministry is about us personally having a relationship with God and from that naturally sharing it. It's critical as we are developing in prophetic ministry that we are authentic and genuine. This comes from being secure in our calling of being the prophet or prophetess. Our confidence must come from knowing who we are and whose we are.

4. LEARN HOW TO BE AN ENCOURAGER

"But the one who prophesies speaks to people for their strengthening, encouraging and comfort (1 Cor 14:3)." Most of the now generation prophets learn first how to be the encourager. Prophetic ministry is primarily one of encouragement, comfort and exhortation (1 Cor. 14:3, Acts 15:32) as seen in the New Testament. Prophets must learn how to master this especially when we are starting out. Prophetic ministry should be reflecting the heart of the Father as Jesus expressed Him.

As prophets grow in your prophetic ministry, God will give you an opportunity to share words that address spiritual warfare or sin. You must prove that you are trustworthy—that you can nurture such words in prayer and submit in an attitude of love and humility.

5. HONOR ALL LEADERS, REGARDLESS OF HOW YOU FEEL ABOUT

THEM.

'Have confidence in your leaders and submit to their authority, because they keep watch over you as those who must give an account. Do this so that their work will be a joy, not a burden, for that would be of no benefit to you (Heb. 13:17)."

A 'prophetic' mentor or, local church leaderships all require honor which is an important aspect of accountability God uses some leaders to grow us in our character and gift and they may not necessarily have prophetic gifts. Having the right attitude towards prophetic accountability and implementing it into your ministry, will break through any limitation on your gift and ministry.

6. LOVE THE WEAPON OF YOUR WARFARE GOD'S WORD

'I run in the path of your commands, for you have broadened my understanding.' (Psalms 119:32)

Those of us who are called to prophetic ministry have a responsibility to know and love God's Word. From the very start, we should be developing a strong foundation in our understanding of the Scripture. There is no excuse for you as a prophet not to study and know the word of God. Once you have that foundation firmly in place, you can learn about prophetic symbolism in the Bible. The stronger you are in God, the more profound and trustworthy your prophetic insights will be.

How is God calling you? The Apostle Paul was called on the Damascus Road through a direct encounter with the living Christ. So dramatic was that call that he was stricken with temporary blindness (Acts 9:1-9). By contrast, Timothy, his son in the gospel, appears to have been called into full time ministry more mundanely, by the recognition and assignment of the Apostle Paul himself (Acts 16:1-5). God does sometimes call through the voice of humans. This leads to the question: how can I know if God is calling me into full-time ministry? Here are some questions to help any prophet clarify whether the call you are sensing is Christ's call to full time ministry.

1. Does the Holy Spirit's urging in the direction of Prophetic Ministry seem more pressing and real?

2. Is the question of the Prophetic call persistent? When the Lord calls, he makes his voice heard with certain persistence.

3. Does the Lord CONFIRM his call by the comments or questions of others? Someone may ask, "Have you ever considered prophetic ministry?"

4. When you are given OPPORTUNITY to serve, do you sense the Lord's blessing in that experience? Do other believers notice it?

5. Do certain areas that the Lord sends across YOUR path fill you with thoughts of a SPECIAL ministry?

6. Do you see needs that you sense you could meet? Some full time ministries have developed simply out of a believer's awareness of

need accompanied by that believer's willingness to attempt to meet that need. That kind of signal is <u>ENHANCED</u> when others also recognizes it.

There is a corporate ladder in the ministry world. We see many now generation prophets are attempting try to climb it, seeking the notoriety. So prophets, ask yourself these 2 questions?

1. Why do you want to ENTER full time prophetic ministry?

2. Why in the world would you leave your current life and CAREER to serve ungrateful sheep, face financial difficulty, suffer biting criticism, be lied to and lied on, endure long hours and short vacations and see your life turned upside down over and over?

But then you could ask, the same question of a full time prophet seeking secular work. The two worlds are more alike than you think. It seems that on either side of the fence, the greener grass loses its luster the longer you stand on it.

Picture yourself several years into full time prophetic ministry. Let one of your worst be days when a subordinate OPENLY undermines your leadership, and see if you still love your job. Most of us who have worked in the secular world or are still working had plenty of similar days.

Know YOUR reasons why and don't assume you heard God call you today then blindly jump tomorrow because chances are great you may be called but not ready to function. Here prophet, are some good reasons and not so good reasons. Judge for yourself. You have to know God has called you! You must be honest with yourself.

1.You want to feel good about your work. Good or Bad for your prophet?

2.You feel the need to please someone else (family, friends, etc.). Good or Bad prophet?

3.You dream of "changing the world." Good or Bad prophet?

4.You failed at other jobs and want to try something new. Good or Bad prophet?

5. You want a CAREER" in the church. Good or Bad prophet?

6.You're low on funds and think church work would be easy money for a while. Good or Bad prophet?

7.You think ministry seems like the most fun job out of several you're considering. Good or Bad prophet?

8.You want to try your hand at full-time ministry to see if you like it. Good or Bad prophet?

9. You see an OPEN church position that has better hours, benefits, or salary than your current position. Good of Bad prophet?

Prophet, you must know what season you are in. While none of us can guess at God's reasons for his timing, God has ordained a place in time for everything. Ecclesiastes 3:1 says,"There is a season for everything, and a time for every activity under heaven." Is a season about to end or BEGIN in YOUR life? Or is the time not yet ripe for any changes?

Prophet, hear this if you hear nothing else: if we would only trust that the Lord brought us into our current season for a limited time to learn specific lessons, to grow in our walk, to serve certain assigned people, We can have faith that our Father in heaven will carry us into the next chapter of our lives at just the right time. This is the key to bloom where you're planted. Every prophet who desires full time ministry must should Test your Ministry with the crossover method. Ministries and churches need people like you.

First, by simply asking how you can help can serve can help you on the path toward your future to full time ministry with incredible speed and precision.

This is what we are doing here in Where Eagles Fly Fellowship Inc. We utilize this method. Right now take inventory of your past experiences since you have been connected and see if you line up.

Second, learn how to volunteer at your or a church, or fellowship with someone's ministry. Increase your involvement to get a taste of more intense service that helps prepare you for full-time ministry work. Here are a few ideas to get you started as you sit down with your pastor, elders, or other volunteers:

- greet visitors

- serve communion

- visit the sick in hospitals

- serve in the nursery

- teach Sunday school

- work with youth

- assist your pastor with sermon research

Prophets, don't rush in; learn about different areas of ministry and experience them. Give time for God to grow you as you learn about yourself. After getting some experience with other areas then you are ready to move forth to your specialized areas of ministry. In other words now you have the foundation to enhance your gift. Prophets, you must do these 20 things. They are critical.

1. Develop an intimate relationship with God and learn to know His voice.

2. Develop your personal Prophets Red list. (The Red File is a personal Prophetic file that my office has developed for our ⍰ prophets that we will make available to those who request.

3. Have a heart to fulfill God's kingdom vision and your destiny.

4. Know your identity in God. Know you are a Prophet and act like it. Don't get frustrated or let people frustrate you while you're trying to make it happen. Put your hand to what is already in front of you, study to show yourself approved and enjoy where you are on the way to where you're going.

5. Get a core group of people around you who believe in you and who will support and pray for you. This is so critical. Know who your core group of people are. Sometimes it takes years to build the right relationships but know they are worth it.

6. Do not be diverted from your call by circumstances or people who don't line up with it. Be sensitive to ungodly counsel.

7. Find a mentor who has experience, who believes in you and your potential, and who is willing to provide the necessary training and equipping to help you fulfill God's call on your life.

8. Go to places where the Spirit of God is moving and get around people who are anointed, particularly in the areas in which you feel called, so you can receive an impartation from them.

9. Attend intense apostolic and prophetic training events.

10. Become a student of the lives of people who have gone before you in ministry, including men and women in the Bible, to learn from their experience.

11. Prepare in every area of your life to pursue God's call. Be ready, LEARN the principles of money, physically prepare yourself, mentally, emotionally equipping must take place and know it is a continual process. And spiritually know what God is asking you to do.

12. Remember that ministry comes out of relationship. CONTINUALLY seek to deepen your relationship with God through prayer and study of the Word.

13. Have a clear understanding of what ministry is. Ministry is simply helping somebody with the love of Jesus wherever there's a need.

14. Don't neglect your family. Take care of your husband, wife, children and responsibilities at home.

15. Don't become a prima donna. Remain touchable and teachable, but guard your Anointing.

16. Make sure you don't hold any bitterness in your heart toward men.

17. Do what you do with excellence.

18. Be Accountable

19. Grow in authority by CONTINUALLY obeying God.

20. Do 1-19 over and over again, if you want to be full time in the Prophetic ministry.

CHAPTER SIXTEEN

As A Prophet Thinketh: Mentality For A New Season

PRACTICAL WAYS PROPHETS BECOME, MENTALLY TOUGH

"Mentally, Are You Ready?"

In The Gospel of today, there are four kinds of prophets you can't help. No matter what you do, or how hard you try there are four kinds of prophets you can't help.

1. You can't help a prophet who does know and refuses to acknowledge or believe he or she has a problem.

2. You can't help a prophet who feels you are the problem.

3. You can't help a prophet who comes to you for direction and they have a better solution than you do.

4. You can't help a prophet who reject sound biblical principles based on the Word of God.

Prophets, understand that you're a champion for God, and we must think as champions. Champions think differently. Five-fold ministry gifts think differently and let there be no doubt that prophets think and process differently. Prophets are unique thinkers within themselves and how they process information. Observe us and this will be become obvious!

When we look at the 'best of the best' or anyone who is relevant in any chosen profession, you see mental toughness. If you've ever watched an athlete like Michael Jordan, Sidney Crosby, or Tiger Woods put on a display of mental toughness, you know this to be true. But while they chat in interviews about the importance of the mental strength, they rarely disclose their actual methods.

This assigned chapter is to enlighten you as a prophet of how to mentally prepare for a new season. Proverbs 23:7 "For as he thinketh in his heart, so is he: Eat and drink, saith he to thee; but his heart is not with thee." Why do athletes under-perform and lose? The same reason prophets and gifted people never really reach their potential or move toward their destiny?

To truly reach your potential in life and shine under any pressure, the first thing you must do is understand why we fail. The reason this happens to most of us as prophets is because we are mentally unprepared for our now season, much less our new season. This is why we see prophets who are afraid. Timid prophets who want to be known but do not want the responsibilities and obligations of carrying such weigh prophetically. The question is "What are we processing and thinking about that encourages us to think defeated and not walk in our calling and destiny?"

Let's look at an athlete to get an idea of mentality. "A tennis player first confronts the Inner Game when he discovers there is an opponent inside his own head more formidable than the one across the net. He then realizes that the greatest difficulty in returning a deep backhand lies not in the speed and placement of the ball itself, but in his mind's reaction to that ball: his own thinking makes the shot more difficult than it really is. For example, your mind is screaming, "You're probably going to miss this one. You'd better get your racket back earlier and make sure to meet the ball out front. If I miss, I'll be down 5-3 on his serve." If thoughts like this are occupying the mind, the ball will appear to approach much faster than it is and will not be seen clearly. Your stroke will be too tight and too contrived to be either effective or fun." It's the classic dilemma.

If you're confronted and doubt who you are, who you're called to be then you're going to be like the tennis player as your mind (the inner voice) will always have you confused. You will always want to doubt it. Prophets, when you over-think and/ or over-analyze, you fail to see things in a 360 degree angle. Fear, anxiety, or nerves interfere with our performance of the execution of our prophetic assignments? To become a mentally tough prophet in this new season, we must start by understanding what's making you afraid in the first place.

Most of us are afraid because we have been programmed by churches, spiritual leaders, parents, and peers that we need to be blessed with three necessary things:

1. Being able to perform well in the opinion of others and ourselves.

2. Winning based on special interest Body of Christ groups.

3. Being confident.

There is nothing wrong with wanting these three things. The problem is that you cannot control any of them. It's really important to know this. You cannot control any of these things. If you as a prophet could control how God uses you then you'd perform to everybody's expectations, you'd always give a peak performance. If you could control winning, you'd always win. If you could control how you feel, you'd always feel confident out there. If you are obsessed with something you cannot control, you will feel scared and anxious all the time.

Prophets learn this: fear and bad nerves do not make for great performance because when it's strong, it interferes with our ability to trust ourselves. One of the world's greatest singers said, "All my life, I wanted to be a great singer. I have spent more money on voice lessons than anything else." Eventually, this singer realized the main reason he was not the singer he wanted to be was that "my desire to sing well was so strong that it had caused my mind to hold my voice hostage.

When I sang, instead of just letting my voice go and simply singing, my mind would try to help my voice to sing. I recognized that, in fact, my voice always knew within itself how to sing. It was my mind that did not know how to sing. As soon as I released my mind from the effort of trying to sing, my voice was freed instantly."

What makes this a vicious cycle for a prophet is that the more you try to control how God will use you and how you look to someone else by performing well, winning, and being confident, the worse you perform, and the more afraid you become. Prophets, your relationship with God must become profound, and relevant. There is no substitute for this.

How do prophets master this concept? There are the courageous self-verses; the coward self.

Become aware of your courageous self. To trigger your courageous self, you must understand your two selves: a courageous warrior self and a coward self. In Joshua chapter 1, God spoke to Joshua at least three times to be strong and be of good courage.

Your courageous self is an aggressive, take-no-prisoners side of you with the Will to Win. When your courageous self is in charge, you are ready for the challenge. As a prophet you must know that challenges are going to happen, and you're willing to face it. In other words, you won't run from the challenges of life in the new season of _____ and you will be able to truly be a front line soldier for God. This was a new season for Joshua, and now it's a new season for each of you!

Whatever God requires, physical, emotional, or financial sacrifice, or even punishment, you're happy to oblige. If God requires that you go outside your comfort zone, you'll do it, and trust him. When your courageous self is in charge, you are highly aware (in tune with) everything that is going on around you, and you adjust in a fraction of a second to what's going on.

For the prophet, your coward self is timid and likes to play it safe. Your coward self will not allow God to be in control and moves in a constant spirit of fear. He or she fears mistakes and does not want to move to one side or the other. Your coward self will only do moves, shots, and patterns inside your comfort zone and feels 100% sure of. It wants to be in control. Sometimes your coward self even tries to "hide" in the middle of conflict hoping no one will notice! Prophets you can't run from conflict in this new season.

As a Prophetic exercise for—YOUR COURAGEOUS SELF
The next step to shining under the pressure that God will put you under is to be consistent in your faith as you get to know

your courageous self really well. Reread Joshua Chapter 1 again. Prophets, please answer the following questions honestly:

1. Name the last assignment you had from God that mattered to you in which you performed really well:

2. Write down three things you did that were coura- geous (you had to do something difficult, and you did it). Did you push yourself through the wall physically, emo- tionally, financially? Were you especially aggressive?

a. _____

b. _____

c. _____

Prophets, keep in mind that you activate your courageous side in the midst of conflict, issues of life. Prophet you must create a sense of CONTROL as control is the step of faith we must learn to operate in that studies and guides us. Most of your fear stems from wanting things we can't control (winning, perform- ing well, being confident).

7 THINGS YOU WANT TO DO IN THE NEW SEASON

#1 STOP PRESSING AND WORRYING

Like athletes, most prophets are obsessed with performing well.

Prophets constantly think about how to perform well and how they may look to someone in the Kingdom of God. Maybe you've been there yourself, we all have. Many times the problem is, when you get obsessed with being a prophet instead of a servant of God, you try to control it. That leads to PRESSING and worry. Pressing/Worrying is the opposite of trusting yourself and the process that God is taking you through. When you press, you're subconsciously trying to force an outcome. You interfere with the process instead of letting God lead.. Stop trying to control the outcome as pressing and worrying will not work in this new season. Moving in control, hearing God in the situation, will bring out your Courageous Self. Instead of PRESSING and worrying, allow your confidence to give you control because your goal is NOT to control something (winning) that cannot be controlled.

Your goal is to come up with several reasons to believe in yourself using the question, "Why Not Me?"

Prophetic EXERCISE—WHY NOT ME?

Write down the name of your latest assignment from God:

_____

_____

b. Write down your goal for this assignment:

c. List at least FIVE believable reasons that answer the question "Why Not Me?"

#2 HOW TO CALM YOUR NERVES AND CRUSH IT IN TRYOUTS

To be a star athlete, you must know in your heart that you CRUSH a team try out or qualifying event when necessary. Remember, the method for mastering fear and triggering your Courageous Self is to create a sense of CONTROL over what you are doing.

The way to take control and turn them from bad nerves into good nerves is actually quite easy. It's called setting a GOAL for your work for God. Remember in pressure situations, your anxiety goes up, and your awareness goes down a bit. This works like a charm because you're not trying to accomplish something that is outside your control. You simply execute your faith and work towards a goal that appears to be one you can't accomplish by yourself, but with God you know you can accomplish it. The "Moses to Pharaoh saga", was such a case. In Exodus 3 we see Moses calming his nerves as the magnitude of his assignment was revealed.

#3 CONTROL WHEN ALL YOU'RE THINKING ABOUT IS YOURSELF "

Prophet, you will never fulfill your destiny by thinking about what God has given you to do. Thinking about what God has given you to do is only a problem if you focus on the merit of it, about whether or not to do it. That's because you cannot control God. If you could, you'd always do only what you want to do. The prophet Jonah being sent to the people of Nineveh is a classic example.

#4 HOW TO NOT BE OVERWHELMED

To be a truly confident, mentally tough prophet you need to know that you are not going to be overwhelmed, because you know who you are and God has called you as a prophet, and not you yourself. You believe in yourself. Ninety seven percent of athletes and specialists in their fields who become overwhelmed never realize or find the reason why they got nervous and choked or became overwhelmed. Most of the time we don't want to face the reasons why, and many times we are under prepared mentally because of something we will not let go of in our past. We take it in our future and it steals our future. When you get scared/overwhelmed, prophet, you need to figure out WHY you're so scared. Something is happening out there that's making you that way. Prophets remember Job.

Once Job trusted God in his stress he got, his power is back. Job was now in a position to solve the problem (Job 42). This mentality brings out your Courageous Side and sheds light on what's kept you from winning. This is actually something you can do, so you're officially back in control.

Prophetic EXERCISE

Write down the last time you feel you were overwhelmed in an assignment that mattered to you: _____

_____

_____

_____

Write down the reason WHY you were over-whelmed, making mistakes, or just not performing:

_____

_____

_____

_____

_____

_____

#5 ACCEPTING YOURSELF UNCONDITIONALLY

Most people, to include prophets, believe (mistakenly) that people that God uses are very self-critical and "hard on them-selves." The truth is that people who God uses are extremely self-supportive. Moses, Joseph, Abraham, Elijah, Elisha, all fit this mode. They may be hard on themselves when it comes to behaviors under their control (such as training hard), but when it comes to their fears, they are quite self-accepting.

Prophets learn how to face your frustrations by putting them into a mental Black Box as you give them to God and never think about them and focus on God.. The faster you learn how to deal with them, the more mentally tough you will be. Facing fear and frustration is the essence of self-acceptance.

Prophets, such self-awareness is powerful. It allows you to DIAGNOSE the root cause of your anxiety so you can execute Gods PRESCRIBED solution for it.

#6 BECOME TOUGH:

To transform yourself into a relevant vessel for God, learn how to manage your expectations for each assignment from God. God's toughest prophets expect major bumps along the way, as they understand its part of the process. It's part of the war, because we have an opponent who hates the prophet. Moses understood this well, and he never stopped. The expectations of the Prophet Elijah were exposed. He learned how to manage his expectations once he went through his ordeal with the evil messenger which landed him in a cave. He learned some things about himself as great as he was!

#7 A DEADLY MINDSET THAT WILL CRUSH OPPONENTS OF YOUR ASSIGNMENT.

The most deadly mindset in sport—one that will make you virtually invincible and able to crush opponents - is to focus completely in the now. Scripture says "Now Faith" (Hebrews 11:1). Now is in in the present moment. Prophets, bringing your focus into the Now brings out your Courageous Self because the only way your mind can create fear is to think about the past failures or the future, you can't control either. This type of mindset will make you to become impervious to distractions. Prophets, you must realize many times why you are criticized; it is often done because it gives people a feeling of importance. It means you are accomplishing something and are worthy of attention." Prophets you must be impervious to criticism.

Prophets, you'll want to avoid THREE colossal mental mistakes that are easy to make when someone is rejecting you in this new season!

Mistake #1: The first mistake is always assuming that the problem is always someone other than you. You must be willing to look at yourself and admit your responsibility and do some mental training to fix it. This is hard to do when all you're thinking about is the other person and not yourself, prophets.

Mistake #2: The second mistake is that you were trying harder to IMPRESS someone else than you were to reach your own goals. Of course, this means you have given someone other than God control and that always leads to PRESSING, which it alone will kill your confidence.

Mistake #3: The third mistake is that you're looking for your hatter's approval. You're a human being. Other people are going to affect you. So here's the question: "Why is it okay for you to reject them, but not for them to reject YOU?" Remember, if you don't like another person or you're rejecting something about him, he KNOWS it. You don't have to tell him that you're not cool with certain things about him especially a discerning anointed prophet. He/She is "picking up what you're putting down" in the energy field.

Prophets, people don't respond to us based on how wonderful we are. They respond to us based on how they feel in our presence. It does not matter how great you are. So many of us never learn this.

Prophets, as long as you are withholding acceptance from God, He isn't going to give you the needed tools of developing your mentality for the new season, because you are rejecting God and his gift upon your life.

You can't have your cake and eat it too. The key to preventing losing in the new season is to have a specific, effective mental toughness in each situation. Jeremiah chapter #1: one of the most important elements of becoming an effective prophet is to operate in the NOW, even if you don't have prophet to the nations aspirations.

CHAPTER SEVENTEEN

Prophetic Awakening

"When You Really, Realize You Are A Prophet"

Prophetic awakening what is it? Consider it waking up to the truth of your knowing that you are a prophet. For most of us, 95% of our energy is spent defending, protecting and maintaining our self-image, and it's all an image: imagination! Prophet, when you ask yourself, "Who am I?" understand that you are your awareness and therefore, you are left with yourself when you ask, "Who am I?". Your calling must be first realized within you!

Your mind always seeks something concrete out of that but there's nothing concrete about our true nature because it is not something that comes and goes like matter. This is a spirit-consciousness of a prophet. Remember, prophet, God is a Spirit, and we worship him in spirit and in truth. Our spirit-consciousness produces thoughts out of itself and we live from these thoughts (beliefs, ideas, conditioning, imagination and emotions). We make them so real that we identify totally with them. This is the reality a prophet lives in.

We normally move through this initial state of Prophetic Awareness to Prophetic Presence. It is the essence of being. Therefore prophet, what awakens us from our spiritual sleep is knowing the difference between pure awareness (knowing, you have something from God) and what you are aware-of, which is knowing you have something! Most prophets struggle with this and remain confused, unclear and have a multitude of questions about themselves when they enter into Prophetic Awakening.

We perceive two ways when we read spiritual literature. The Bible, we understand intellectually and emotionally both, creates barriers in our understanding but we must die to both of these as prophets to move in the fullness of what God has called us to be. The Prophetic Awakening develops our Prophetic Mentality.

Prophetic awakenings are timeless. They happen in the moment. They happen now. There's no lead time. There's no post awakening time. Prophetic Awakening is not about the process of making a spiritual experience happen. You are still human after a Prophetic Awakening. Many times prophets think a lot human difficulties would be washed out of this world by being awakened prophetically.

As prophets we still have issues. We will still make mistakes. We love. We will get angry. We will get scared. We will grieve because all of this is part of the great tapestry of human life. It is part of the whole, and awakening has no preference over any other part of our life. It's a confusing and somewhat scary thought.

In general terms, a Prophetic Awakening is an altered state of perception. It is a knowing beyond knowledge. Reality has changed for a prophet who experiences this type of awakening. In short, a Prophetic Awakening is allowing yourself to be open and inviting the living Spirit of God and the love of God to enter your heart. It is the moment when God awakens your soul to a new awareness, a new perception of the world around you and your purpose for your gifting. A Prophetic Awakening is when the confused and frightened budding prophet transcends to a higher consciousness, an awareness full of love and peace.

Prophet, your new responsibilities of Prophetic Awakening must be adhered to. You are the only one in charge of your ministry no matter what year it is or what vortex is opening. You are the only one who can embrace all of you. If you don't do this, no one else will. Prophet If you don't chose to live life from a more conscious and kind awareness every day, no one else will. You are making a choice to live in the new awakening or conciseness.

Prophet, letting go of all unproductive attachments, in your life as you reassert your new conciseness is critical. Prophet, this still always comes back to you. You're in charge of you. So Prophet, if you are waiting on the sidelines for some perfect moment, forget it. Leave this alone. The prophetic water is not what you are expecting. Prophet, you simply have to let go of the idea of the perfect moment, and then jump in.

You can't use the world as an excuse for how you are feeling or if you are ready to awaken. In many respects, awakening is something your soul is already planning to do or not. Still that doesn't mean that there isn't value in preparing yourself for an awakening. How do you do that? You follow your heart. Prophets should make every new year as a reason to make space for more Prophetic Awakenings. Prophets make space for there to be prophetic caretakers to those who have a Prophetic Awakening Anointing. Prophets, we must learn how to make space and have more love in our relationships, so we can grow. Prophetic growth will begin for you when you begin to embody it and live from that space in this world. Bring your hope and your happiness to that very moment. Bring your awareness to this moment. Make the prophetic awakening come true by embracing the fullness of yourself. Joseph showed us this in Genesis 39 and 40.

The prophetic mantle is a heavy mantle; not everyone is cut out to carry it. Elijah didn't offer his prophetic mantle to just anyone; he waited for the right person, Elisha. Elisha was a wealthy man who willingly gave up everything to gain the prophetic mantle. But, Elisha didn't go to Elijah to gain his mantle; he joined the man of God to be close to the man of God. He was hungry for the anointing. In return, Elisha became close to the God the man of God he served as he served Elijah. For some of us our desire for the prophetic mantle began by being attracted to those carrying it.

Something in you wanted to learn of that gift. If we yearn for the prophet, we will gain the prophet's mantle. This is Prophetic Awakening in its purest form. There is a common trend today to minimize the importance of proximity.

Today Prophets have the web, email, voice-mail, Skype, DVD, CD's and a host of other technological wonders. But, these things, as wonderful as they are, cannot replace the power of being present. The anointing is caught more than it is taught. To catch the prophetic mantle, we must be with the prophet. If you're not willing to pay the price you can't expect the benefits of the gift. Again you must be there and there is no way of getting around this.

This can be difficult. Prophets often have very visible personality flaws. Prophets are flawed on purpose. Their flaws are usually great. The greater the prophetic mantle on a prophet, the greater the flaws in the prophet. Why? Humility. Humility is the key to gaining and walking in the prophetic mantle. True prophets are humble and flawed human beings.

Those of you who want to be awaken prophetically after you have come in covenant with a prophet listen closely. To gain the prophetic mantle, we must push past the prophet's flaws. Sometimes, this means getting into the mud with the prophet. When Elijah crossed Jordan, Elisha was with him, and he wouldn't leave him, even if it meant getting his feet muddy. Elijah was a tough mentor. Elijah was in tune with God. Elijah called others to focus on God. This was his calling. His calling often caused him to lose sight of others: their needs, their pains, their struggles. Elijah was hard on Elisha. Elisha endured Elijah: he pressed past Elijah's flaws to gain Elijah's mantle. Elisha desired Elijah's mantle. Elisha was willing to do what was necessary to gain Elijah's mantle. Elisha became God's prophet by being with God's prophet - Elijah. Elisha gained Elijah's mantle. Elisha, after receiving Elijah's mantle, tested it. Elisha put Elijah's God to the test. The test question: where is the Lord God of Elijah? This question set the stage for the new prophet, Elisha. This is a new awakening if you can pass the test.

When God sets a stage for you, don't draw back, or run from it. You move towards it. Take up the prophetic mantle, and carry it. Use it to glorify God so that a clarion sound of the prophetic voice can be heard. The prophetic mantle is awakened. The prophet's mantle must be passed. Today's prophets need the anointed mantle of the prophet passed to them by yesterday's prophets so that they can begin bearing fruit and bringing forth the blessing of genuine prophecy to a new generation. Today's prophets can enter in to the greater blessings that genuine prophecy brings if they are willing to let senior prophets teach them their revelation of realms of prophetic ministry.

True prophetic ministry is defined by two important words that enlighten us to Prophetic Awakening:

1) Humility... Elijah and Elisha

2) Teachability. Genuine prophetic ministry begins with humility and is maintained by being teachable.

Prophets, keeping yourselves humble and teachable opens the door for the greater blessings of God through genuine prophetic ministry.

Prophets, if you want the blessing of genuine prophetic ministry, and the prophet's mantle, then you must walk in humility and being teachable. This type of awakening will either move to towards the kingdom or away from it. There is no more middle ground. No compromise. No independent of the purposes of God left to pretend. You will either be for Him or against Him. Many well-meaning prophets of the God, will find themselves faced with a choice. That choice will mean GLORY or DESTRUCTION.

Prophets are not always the most popular five-fold ministry gift holders on the block because they are bold enough to release a word of the Lord that deals with sin or that warns the local church of potentially unpleasant circumstances coming down the proverbial pike. In order to properly carry this mantle, genuine prophets must build towers of prayer. False prophets build walls of religion that lead people astray with fabricated edification, misleading exhortation and counterfeit comfort.

Ezekiel 13:10 says, "Tell these white washers that their wall will soon fall down". Verily, verily, the whitewashed walls of religion are going to come tumbling down in a heap of self-righteous rubble and the false prophets are coming down right along with them. True prophets may not always have the flare, charisma or appeal, but who said they are supposed to? Jeremiah wasn't the most popular prophet in his time, nor was Ezekiel in his day.

John the Baptist had his head served up on a silver platter for warning the people of the looming decision between everlasting life and eternal hell fire. But they were the unadulterated mouthpieces of God. They had been enlightened and awakened.

The result of Prophetic Enlightenment for prophets, by contrast, may not win any popularity contests in the local church, but they will sacrifice to make intercession. Instead of building walls of religion, they build towers of prayer; watchtowers in the spirit that allow them to see the assignments coming against the local church. They take that revelation and use it as spiritual mortar to make up a hedge in prayer.

You can't separate a prophet from prayer any more than you can separate an evangelist from preaching the Gospel. The very first time you ever see the word "prophet" in the Bible, it is connected to prayer. In the book of Genesis, when Abimelech took Abraham's wife, the Lord said, "Now return the man's wife, for he is a prophet, and he will pray for you and you will live." (Genesis 20:7) So while not every intercessor is a prophet, every prophet is an intercessor.

Let's talk about the functions of Prophetically Awakened Prophets. Prophets are often called watchmen. Scripture reveals three types of prophetic sentinels whose mission is to stand guard, keep watch and report what they see. We find Old Testament prophets on the walls, walking in the streets of the city and in the countryside.

"I have set watchmen upon thy walls, O Jerusalem, which shall never hold their peace day nor night: ye that make mention of the Lord, keep not silence." (Isaiah 62:6) Watchmen on the walls are positioned to see far distances in the spirit and discern whether friend or foe is approaching. The watchman gives word to those in authority so they can decide whether to sound an alarm of welcome or an alarm of war. In today's local church, these prophetic watchmen help protect against enemy attacks. Every prophet is called to this post.

Today we have prophets who has been called to The Nations and have been prophetically awakened. These are those prophets in the harvest fields of the world. Prophets sent to the nations have a clear role in Prophetic Evangelism as watchmen who protect the people against the destructive work of principalities and powers that keep the lost from hearing the truth.

Prophets should be deployed on local church outreaches and international missions to watch, guard, pull down and destroy opposition to the Word of God. "The watchmen found me as they made their rounds in the city (Song of Solomon 3:3; 5:7)." In today's times, this watchman, the prophet to the nation is assigned to stand guard over the Body of Christ to see emerging problems. This is a larger responsibility that carries with it a heavier prayer burden and greater implications for the Church at large. Anyone carrying a prophetic mantle needs to closely examine the fruit of his or her ministry.

7 SIGNS OF PROPHETIC AWAKENING

There are seven signs of a Prophetic awakening:

1) Spiritual uneasiness, dissatisfaction with your state of spirituality;

2) You will experience the enlightenment of the Spirit coming upon you, enlightening your existence;

3) The consciousness of work for others, not for our own only; a sense of mission;

4) The shouting of danger heard by our spirit now alerts you as a prophet to threats you have never been aware of.

5) There is an initiative of others in spiritual awakening; as you sense their issues.

6) The feeling of spiritual hunger or spiritual thirst, now shadows you as you spirit becomes hungry for better values in life; and

7) The desire to contemplate the spiritual beauty within you now grows as you desire the anointing upon your life to rest there.

Do not be a foolish prophet and build your ministry on the sands of seduction for the sake of acceptance because God promises that rain will pour from the heavens, hailstones will come hurtling down and violent winds will burst forth against those whitewashed walls and expose them (Ezekiel 13:11-12).

Instead, build your ministry on the Word of God and prophesy the mind of Christ so that when the hurricanes of religion come against the local church and when Jezebel hurls her spiritual sleet at the sanctuary, and when the winds of witchcraft blow against the walls, the foundation of your ministries and any church assigned to you will be fortified to stand and withstand in the day of battle.

CHAPTER EIGHTEEN

A Closing Thought

"The Season Of Now And Beyond"

The very sound of negative words and thoughts were what inspired me to learn more and not allow myself to take anyone or anything for granted. I'm so glad I did. I tapped into God's revelation knowledge and you can to. This work is not intended to impress you. It is intended to empower you.

Today we see much in the news and media about men and women of God. To put it bluntly, it is not even close to being good. When there is news or reports of a prophet, or even an apostle, it has a doubling effect upon the body of Christ and the perception of the foundation gifts of the church. We have a responsibility to empower and educate. We may not all know each other, but we can by our work become the prophetic stewards that God called us to be in this generation. We have ample room to grow and improve. Greatness is still available.

I humbly and strongly suggest that you find you a prophetic home and become empowered. Home is home and you're always going to have some bumps and bruises, but the enemy we face is moving rapidly in and out of our ranks and is set to destroy us at specific times. I'm excited to say, here at Where Eagles Fly, we are building a prophetic company for prophets and prophetic people. Every prophet will not fit in WEF, nor do we expect that. We are an example of what God can do, in the midst of haters, backstabbers and ditch diggers. Look at us. We continue to soar with the Eagles. We thank God every day. Prophet, find you a home. It does not have to be WEF. It simply has to be your prophetic home!

We have the victory and no matter how rough it gets, and it can get rough, know that God has someone, somewhere who sees that you're in the wilderness and will bring you through the experience as we do have much work to do. Thank you for reading this book, I pray you see things differently now and understand this is only the beginning. I look forward to sharing with you again in The Wilderness Prophet II. We have much work to do.

Contact me through my website at www.whereeaglesfly. us or call my office at 919-695-3375 or 919-213-1328. I'm on

Facebook under my name and watch Live video teachings on The Prophets Teaching Group and Periscope under my name.

Blessings

Apostle Ken Cox

Where Eagles Fly

About The Author

Apostle Ken Cox started serving God in 1994 after a series of unforeseen life failures. Out of the military and seemly starting life over again, by 2000, Apostle Cox had found his life calling as a Prophet. The challenge of learning and understanding presented a new frontier. Apostle Cox dove into the process and has now emerged as a well-traveled prophet who serves the Body of Christ as an Apostle.

Apostle Cox, along with his wife, Prophetess Sabina Cox are the leaders of Where Eagles Fly Fellowship Inc., a fellowship of prophets and apostle across the USA and beyond who are dedicated and focused on establishing the prophetic gift back into society as they raise up prophets around the country and abroad.

Apostle Cox and Prophetess Cox are available for Revivals, Conferences and Meetings. They have been featured in meetings and sought-after to teach and instruct the prophetic for ministries seeking to learn more about the gift.

Apostle and Prophetess Cox have 3 children and 4 grandkids as of this writing and currently reside in Durham, NC. Contact them through the Where Eagles Fly office at 919-695-3375 or 919-213-1328 or at www.whereeaglesfly.us.

References

1. prophetic. (n.d.). Dictionary.com Unabridged. Retrieved June 30, 2017 from Dictionary.com website http://www.dictionary.com/browse/prophetic

2. prophecy. (n.d.). Dictionary.com Unabridged. Retrieved June 30, 2017 from Dictionary.com website http://www.dictionary.com/browse/prophecy

3. prophet. (n.d.). Dictionary.com Unabridged. Retrieved June 30, 2017 from Dictionary.com website http://www.dictionary.com/browse/prophet

4. Rory (2006) Fatigue Makes Cowards Of Us All. Retrieved June 30, 2017 from website http://chirontraining.blogspot.com/2006/01/fatigue-makes-cowards-of-us-all.html

5. G1383 - dokimion - Strong's Greek Lexicon (KJV). Retrieved from   https://www.blueletterbible.org//lang/lexicon/lexicon.cfm?Strongs=g1383&t=kjv

6. "Discern." Merriam-Webster.com. Merriam-Webster, n.d. Web. 30 June 2017.

7. G1253 - diakrisis - Strong's Greek Lexicon (KJV). Retrieved from   https://www.blueletterbible.org//lang/lexicon/lexicon.cfm?Strongs=G1253&t=KJV

8. G2296 - thaumazō - Strong's Greek Lexicon (KJV). Retrieved from   https://www.blueletterbible.org//lang/lexicon/lexicon.cfm?Strongs=g2296&t=kjv

9. G1605 - ekplēssō - Strong's Greek Lexicon (KJV). Retrieved from   https://www.blueletterbible.org//lang/lexicon/lexicon.cfm?Strongs=G1605&t=KJV

10. G3140 - martyreō - Strong's Greek Lexicon (KJV). Retrieved from https://www.blueletterbible.org//lang/lexicon/lexicon.cfm?Strongs=G3140&t=KJV

11 G32 - aggelos - Strong's Greek Lexicon (KJV). Retrieved from https://www.blueletterbible.org//lang/lexicon/lexicon.cfm?Strongs=G32&t=KJV

12. 4397. malak Strong's Concordance Retrieved July 1, 2017 from http://biblehub.com/hebrew/4397.htm

CPSIA information can be obtained
at www.ICGtesting.com
Printed in the USA
FSOW03n0340060218
44064FS